POETRY
To
PONDER

REX B. VALENTINE

Poetry To Ponder by Rex B. Valentine

This book is written to provide information and motivation to readers. Its purpose is not to render any type of psychological, legal, or professional advice of any kind. The content is the sole opinion and expression of the author, and not necessarily that of the publisher.

Copyright © 2018 by Rex B. Valentine

All rights reserved. No part of this book may be reproduced, transmitted, or distributed in any form by any means, including, but not limited to, recording, photocopying, or taking screenshots of parts of the book, without prior written permission from the author or the publisher. Brief quotations for noncommercial purposes, such as book reviews, permitted by Fair Use of the U.S. Copyright Law, are allowed without written permissions, as long as such quotations do not cause damage to the book's commercial value. For permissions, write to the publisher, whose address is stated below.

Printed in the United States of America.

ISBN 978-1-949746-22-8 (Paperback)
ISBN 978-1-949746-23-5 (Digital)

Lettra Press books may be ordered through booksellers or by contacting:

Lettra Press LLC
18229 E 52nd Ave.
Denver City, CO 80249
1 347-903-4909 | info@lettrapress.com
www.lettrapress.com

TABLE OF CONTENTS

Dedication vii
Acknowledgements ix
Foreword xiii
Introduction xv

When You Were A Child 1
The Man I Want To Be 2
Plan For Success 3
Dessert First 4
A Wish Or A Prayer? 4
Perfect Communication 5
Tell A Vision 6
The Answer To Peace In The World 7
The Cows Are Out! The Cows Are Out! 8
The Medicare Band 10
The Simple Prayer 12
The Test 12
Cycles Of War 13
Excuse? Live On Stage 13
A Dog Named Bob 14
About Conan 16
Defy Enmity 17
Where Is Peace? 17
Crosby's Slaughterhouse 18
Remarkable Nonsense 19
There Will Be A Brighter Day 20
Those Dirty Swimmers 21
Twenty Seasons In A Year? 22
Unforgettable Seventy-Fifth Birthday 23
Who Were Those Who Kept The Faith? 24

Sow With Love	25
Wisdom	26
The Beach Vendors Of Mexico	27
Observations Of A Poet	28
Giving	29
Stuck With Sticks	29
Open Doors	30
Precious Water	31
Discipline And Love Conquers Self	32
Dad's Dirty Rag	34
Just Waiting	35
Dear Auntie Is Older	36
Finding Happiness In Life	37
My Garage, Too Small?	37
The World Of Forgettory	38
Love Is A Road	39
The Valentine Adventure	40
Expectation	41
The Benefactors Of God's Spirit And Love	41
Shopping Crisis	43
My Spirit	43
Dessert----My Greatest Pleasure	45
There Is Power In The Fast	45
Double Talk, Double Rhyme, Spirit Answer	46
Re-Runs In The Theatre Of Life	47
God's Work Must Go On	49
The Waterfall—Remember?	49
Inspiration, Knowledge, Wisdom	50
My Mind, A Mine	51
The Bouquet Of Life	52
The Magical Library	53
Search For The Gold	54
The Tip	55
I Am An Authority	57
The Wonder Of His Power, The Power Of His Word	58
The Waiting Room	59
Harmony	59
Cedar Creek, The Enchanted Stream	60

My Spirit Unchanged	61
Fried Chicken Joy	62
Slipping From Work To Rest	64
Learning To Milk Evangeline	65
The Master-Mind	66
Be My Guest	67
The Babysitter	68
Allergies	68
A Sinner's Lament	70
The Beauty Of A Wave	71
The Miracle Of Music	72
Angel Thoughts	73
Our Fair Feathered Friends In Flight	74
Escape The Honey Doos	75
Hidden Good	76
Matured Nostalgia	77
Obedience Speaks To The Holy Spirit	78
My First Fish	78
Time After Time After Time	80
Attitude	80
Waiting	81
Unraveling Rhyme	82
The "Cow-Tow"	83
Christmas Cheer, Now It's Here	84
Comfort	85
Australian Hsinku	86
Frog Hsinku	86
Why His Song Was Long	86
The House With A Purple Door	87
The Savor Of His Salt	88
Oh Winter Day	89
Deers Is Scared, But Bears Is Not	89
Poet Of Fame	90
Beautiful, I Think	91
Almost Home	92
Jealousy	93
Love Never Faileth	94
A Villanelle! You Can't Tell?	95

The Wonder Of Love	96
Seek Power Of Perpetual Perfection	97
A Blossom Of Spring	98
Music And Flight	99
The Address Book	99
Tell A Vision	101
The Bike With Four Feet	102
Preserve Beauty	103
Hindsight	104
Leadership	104
Persistance	104
The Pruner	105

DEDICATION

This book of original poetry, which I have written and produced through the years is hereby dedicated to my wonderful grandmother, Laura Jane (Ridings) Easter, who inspired me as a child to enjoy stories and descriptions of people, places, and things with poetic beauty. She saw good in simple, everyday experiences and was quite a poet herself. She was born near Porter, WA. in 1878 to James Atwell and Phoebe Jane (Babcock) Ridings, who settled there in 1864 and lived her whole life in that tiny community called Sharon, WA. She married Richard Higgins Easter, a neighbor boy. Her great influence on my mother, Dorothy Estelle (Easter) Valentine, helped my mother kindle the sparks of learning in me as a tiny lad. To them I am eternally grateful.

ACKNOWLEDGEMENTS

My thanks go to my dear wife, Diane E. Valentine, for her ability to listen to my new poems and critique them in a constructive way; at times responding very bluntly if she didn't like a topic, or passage. Also, my secretary, Fran Frazier, put many hours in typing and helping me improve my manuscripts. Daughter-in-law, Barbara Erickson was always ready to proofread the final book form. The book cover photo is by Dr. Russell Valentine and submitted by Carol Valentine.

POETRY STYLES USED IN THIS BOOK

NARRATIVE POETRY: tells a story. There are several main kinds of narrative poetry forms. The poets of old used the ***long verse*** styles such as Henry Wadsworth Longfellow, Will M. Carleton, Robert Service, Ralph Waldo Emerson and many other famous poets. Their stories rhymed and most were metered in various ways. Some stories were quite gruesome and spectacular in the word pictures they painted. Not the least of these was used by Edgar Allen Poe in his "The Raven".

VILLANELLES: are a fixed form of poetry consisting of 19 lines of any length (although many poets also use iambic pentameter or other iambic meters) divided into six stanzas: five tercets (three lines) and one quatrain (4 lines) in the last stanza. The first and third lines of the initial tercet rhyme as do all other tercets (meaning the last words of the lines rhyme). These rhymes are repeated in each subsequent tercet (ABA) and in the final two lines of the quatrain (ABAA). Line 1 reappears in its entirety as lines 6, 12 and 18; while line 3 reappears as lines 9, 15 and 19. All second lines of all stanzas must rhyme also. Line 19 sometimes has a small variation from its former lines, to give more meaning to the ending. The trick is to follow all the rules and still tell the story meaningfully with either a sonnet or villanelle.

SONNETS: having only 14 lines can and were used as narratives. Their verse had a few main rhyming patterns, and most used a meter called iambic. The first syllable unaccented and the second accented, together called a "foot". Most of these sonnets used iambic pentameter, whose lines had ten syllables or five "feet": da DA da DA da DA da DA da DA. Shakespeare was a master of this style, so famous that many of these sonnets are called "Shakespearian Sonnets". The first eight lines set out the story or problem, the next four lines offer a conclusion or solve the problem, and the last two lines, which always rhyme, are called a couplet and put a cap or ending on the story or theme. To tell a story in only 14 lines is not easy. One learns to make a single line pinch-hit for a whole paragraph at times. The most used rhyming patterns are ABAB, CDCD, EFEF, GG; or ABBA, ABBA, CDCD, EE.

The letters refer to the last words on a line, as all "A" words rhyme, all B words rhyme, etc.

FREE VERSE: is much easier to write. It has been used more and more in later years. However, there seems to be a move in some poetry circles to get back to rhyme again. In visiting with Donald Hall in 2004, he expressed his gradual return to more structured verse. (He has since been named as the Poet Laureate of the US, appointed by President G. W. Bush.)

In my opinion, free verse has gotten out of hand. Few of us seem to enjoy the mostly disjointed poems out there. They are very hard to read and understand. There seem to be no rules or norm, and I have found very few who want to keep what is written for future readings.

HAIKU: A Japanese three-line poem of 17 syllables with no rhyming necessary. Generally, the first and last lines have 5 syllables and the middle line has 7 syllables.

HSINKU: Is a four line Chinese poem of any length; the 2nd and 4th lines must rhyme. The 4th line indicates a surprise ending or an unusual twist to the poem's meaning.

FOREWORD

This poem entitled "Grandpa's House" was written by the author's granddaughter, Whitney Seaberg Keith in honor of her Grandpa, Rex B. Valentine, telling about some of her fondest memories on his farm at 144 Hurd Rd., Elma, Washington. She was raised on adjoining property, so spent many hours with her grandparents.

Grandpa's House

The door is always open, grandchildren enter in
For a friendly game of ping-pong, but who is going to win?
Or to sit up at the counter, hot rolls just hit the spot
Or pudding, cakes or cookies, there always was a lot
Hide and seek, a favorite, down the chute we'd go
Shhh…don't' let Grandpa see you, he will never know
Let's make some laps around the loop, let's count them as we run
Is this to get some exercise or is this just for fun?
Out to the barn to jump on bales, and rafters we will swing
There's so much to do at Grandpa's house, we can do anything!
The memories, so vivid, so alive within my mind
Grandpa always with a smile, so gentle and so kind
Many years have passed and I have children of my very own
And I want them to have memories, of this man I've known
So every night, they listen to the Rutabaga Patch
Requesting, "Grandpa Rex", I think they are attached
And Tiddlywinks the 3 eared-horse, they also want to hear
As I sit there reading it, I feel like you are near
Great memories, I have, of Grandma and of You
I hope my children get to make, some great memories too.

Whitney Keith
March 13, 2012

INTRODUCTION

> I am a little spam.
> They cook me in a pan.
> And when I'm done they take me out
> And eat me like a man.

This is one of Rex Valentine's four-year-old attempts at poetry. In other words, he's been at it a long time. Living on a primitive farm, where entertainment was what they made for themselves, his parents fostered creativity through music and writing in their humble home. His grandmother wrote and read her own poems to him during his growing up years, which further inspired him. Despite his penchant for dreaming and using his imagination he was still a red- blooded "skookum" farm boy. (Skookum is an Indian word for strong or stout) He excelled in the major high school sports, of football, basketball, baseball, track and boxing, while still achieving high marks in his subjects and was proud to earn the Valedictorian and Outstanding Musician's Awards for his high school class of 1952. He credits much of his writing skill to the fine teachers he had, especially Mr. John Terry who introduced him to Shakespearian sonnets and encouraged his ability to compose his own sonnets of which he now has 32 to his credit.

In his adulthood, which has spanned more than 60 years, he has worn many hats, raised 11 children, been in more than a few businesses and led an interesting and colorful life. All along the way, he has been recording his life experiences in both prose and poetry. Added to that, he has composed a fine selection of music, some of which is published in a collection of gospel songs and some sheet music for choir use. Since his semi-retirement he's been inducted into the "World Congress of Poets" and his work is now internationally recognized.

Rex has already published two books of poetry. Several others of his publications are also available and include a children's story, "Tiddlywinks

The Little Horse with three Ears", and a book detailing his experiences with water dowsing (one of his businesses of 50 years) entitled "Dowsing Discoveries, Finding Water and Other Mysteries". His works "The Rutabaga Patch" and "Spreading Chestnut Wisdom" are delightful volumes containing rhyming narratives of his childhood adventures and a few from his later life. Written in his unique and exceptional style, he adds interest and authenticity to the stories by personally illustrating them.

This, his most recent book, "Poetry to Ponder", is a little different from his previous works in that it includes some of his sonnets and some non-rhyming poems and villanelles and hsinkus. The diversity of his subjects and style is truly amazing. It also highlights several exceptional poems that garnered 1st place in international contests and others that were judged from second to sixth places. The beauty of Rex's writing lies partly in the fact that it is easy to understand. Yet the work, while retaining its clarity, is still thought provoking and full of meaning, and in many ways becomes a valiant blueprint for the good life. There are no illustrations in this book, but each selection has an introductory remark from the author telling where, when or how it came to be. It is a timeless and pleasant volume that everyone will enjoy.

WHEN YOU WERE A CHILD

Beautiful memories can stay with us a lifetime. These are some of mine. Written on Feb. 28, 2011, while waiting and hoping for an early spring, (which we didn't get) I thought back over my wonderful childhood and remembered many of the scenes of beauty and contentment, and dream times that I experienced. I later added more to the poem.

When you were a child and found a big box
that was empty, but open, without any locks.
Did you want to crawl in and hide their awhile?
shut off from the world? Did you secretly smile?

When you were a child did you climb up a tree,
looking out o'er a field, or the waves of the sea?
Did you revel in sights that seemed endless, then vague?
Did you want to jump out? But it might break your leg?

Have you laid on your back under warm starry skies,
drank awe from the dipper, while a meteor flies?
Have you thought you might taste of the milk in the way
as it flowed through the heavens' in gorgeous array?

When you were a child and played hard all day.
Mom tucked you in bed, with soft pillows. She'd say,
"Sweet dreams, sleep tight, may the Lord bless your night".
Did your consciousness fade into peaceful delight?

Can you put into words the feelings you had
while lying in flowers upon the earth's pad?
Peeking out through the blossoms in a colorful field
thinking no one could see you, as you were concealed?

While watching the heavens, the picture bouquet,
the fluffy white clouds on a warm summer day.
Were there faces and numbers and fairy ballet,
as you fantasized messages, there on display?

Did you climb, pick and eat fresh fruit from your trees?
Or walk through the garden and taste fresh shelled peas?
Or smell new mown hay as it wafted the breeze?
Can you ever forget those sensations that please?

These are the good things our lives bring to pass
like clouds, stars and fruit, and newly mown grass,
clean sheeted soft beds and flowering fields,
and gardens alive with fresh vegetable yields.

Indelible thoughts, impressions we love,
experiences we'll always keep thinking of.
But now we have grown to maturity's peak!
We've put away childish things (so to speak)

We're too big for presents that Santa might bring,
But still hope the mailman will bring us **something**.

When reading this over, I chuckled and smiled.
I hope I will never cease being a child.

THE MAN I WANT TO BE

Written 11/21/07 while flying to Salt Lake to see daughter Anne, Jason and children. This is my true desire. The poem garnered 4th place internationally in the rhyming category of the World Congress of Poets' convention in Greece 2011.

There are those who live their lives as if there was no other.
Their thoughts are only for themselves and seldom for a brother.
They weep with every problem that besets them; what a pity.
To listen to their list of woes would make a person giddy.
At other times with other men, a caring soul emerges
just when one is feeling bad the hurt and pain he purges.
That special soul's appearance may belie his inner grace,

for looks can be deceiving, hence there's more than form or face.
Compassion, love of fellow man flow from his heart and hands.
Just when one thinks that no one cares, he soothes and understands.
Oh, that I can be like he, who thinks of others first.
That I may living waters give when e'er my brothers thirst.
That I may see with heart and soul as well as with my eyes,
to be aware of others' needs, then help, not criticize.
There is a pattern left for us. It's there for all to see.
I pledge to think of others first and last of all, of me.

PLAN FOR SUCCESS
SONNET #20

Make your plans, expecting good outcomes, even if road blocks appear. Written 8/13/04 to encourage myself to not fail if I was careful in planning.

The wise and educated men of old
have given much advice to common man.
Success may come to those in search of gold,
if they who seek devise a perfect plan.

Now, gold is found in many, many forms.
Success to one might be another's lack.
There are no universal plans, or norms,
nor must each road in life be white or black.

However, one should set one's goals high
and spend some time to chart each future course,
expecting, hoping, shooting for the sky,
proceeding forth with faith, and not with force.

One's test is best, when things get out of hand,
but still succeeds, though things don't go as planned.

DESSERT FIRST

A blue ribbon poem in Grange contest 2009 makes sense of wishful thinking.

I prefer to eat dessert first!
Why should I take a chance?
There may not be any left, that's the worst,
and I find there's no recompense,
when it's gone, it's gone,
to be seen no more.
Not even a smell lingers on
like you had before.
Besides, dessert first will help my weight.
No one wants to be skinny.
Then I'll know how much room on my plate
to leave for veggies and fruit, if any.
At a buffet I'm hardly able,
when they push and shove, to be first in line.
So I start at the other end of the table
where the pie and the cake soon are mine.

A WISH OR A PRAYER?
VILLANELLE# 16

This villanelle expressed my feelings and thankfulness for my Heavenly guidance. Written 6/27/08.

Some say a wish can often be a prayer,
if uttered when we're young, or when we're old.
It matters not for Jesus Christ is there.

If we but think of God, Christ is aware
and leads us to the Father as foretold.
Some say a wish can often be a prayer.

If we conclude that we are in despair
and Satan seems to have a stranglehold,
it matters not for Jesus Christ is there

to hear our wishful cry," Does someone care?"
Then God's fair angels act, and us enfold.
Some say a wish can often be a prayer.

His light will shine; our burdens He will share.
When sinful thoughts do threaten us, behold,
it matters not for Jesus Christ is there.

Our God, his loving Son, and angels fair
do watch and guide us as our lives unfold.
Some say a wish can often be a prayer.
It matters not for Jesus Christ is there.

PERFECT COMMUNICATION

Our experiences of the spirit can include animals. Under certain circumstances, they seem to know what we want and can act accordingly.

Old Tag and Nig, Dad's skillful team of horses were the best;
or so he thought, they always seemed one cut above the rest.
Two thousand pounds, a dapple gray, Dad's fav'rite was old Tag.
When pulling heavy loads away his gut would nearly drag.

I watched, though I was just a lad and no experience I had
to judge the feelings of a horse. But when I sensed my Dad enforce
his thoughts and wishes of the course old Tag should pull the wagon through
by softly clucking, whistle sucking, pulling lines, he gave the clue.
So Tag would lead without Nig bucking in the harness as they drew
the wagon 'cross the rushing stream o're slip'ry rocks, his feet were sure,
wide Belgian hooves that gripped, it seemed,

inspiring Nig, though insecure to spawn his best expenditure,
I tuned my spirit to the waves twixt horse and man where faith was king,
exuding secret silent raves. My Dad had hardly said a thing.

Though in my youth, the silent call from man to beast excited me.
I didn't understand it all but knew it wasn't fantasy.
Throughout my life I gently stored connecting silent thoughts so free;
that spirit line, that endless chord that stretches to eternity.

TELL A VISION
VERSION 1

On our church Mission we didn't have the television, so we visited a lot and so enjoyed each other. 2/20/06

Can you "Tell a Vision" of your mind's chromatic screens?
Entwine your mind with others when portraying vivid scenes?

The art of story telling is as varied as the sand.
Some tales may be most interesting when they're told firsthand.

Sometimes it helps, when in bed, to narrate in the dark,
where pictures form within your head from colorful remark.

There is no competition there, from garish shades of light,
so you can "Tell a Vision," color film, or black and white.

Hearts can come together, dreams can be projected then,
without the opposition of a why, or how, or when.

Rivers deep become small streams, steep mountains, gentle slopes.
If there's a tear it can't be seen, but both feel love and hopes.

It may be reminiscing that can take the center stage
with memories so vivid, though attained at early age.

A hero's role you did assume in looking back with pride.
It warms your heart relating how you saved your blushing bride

from certain death when joy-riding in your open Jeep.
Remember, Dear, remember when...Oh rats, she's gone to sleep!

THE ANSWER TO PEACE IN THE WORLD

Most of us dream of world peace. This poem came to me 3/28/04. It was judged 4th place internationally for rhyming poetry in 2009 at Nicaragua.

A world of peace—is it a dream?
Or is it an unattainable theme?

For centuries men have fought to win
a peace that leads to war again.

Contentment fosters apathy,
and riches almost guarantee

that man will conquer man through greed,
and jealousy, mistrust and need.

That theme of peace—most every soul
is pierced at times; has no control,

as worldly pressures push and pull...
that cup of peace is never full.

When will we see that Faith is King;
that love can conquer everything?

That hope is not beyond our grasp
if hands of friendship touch and clasp.

THE COWS ARE OUT!
THE COWS ARE OUT!

Another true story about living on a cattle ranch. I've found we can talk and communicate to our cattle by word and mind. 1/13/02

I heard a car come in our drive
at one o'clock this morn.
I forced myself to come alive,
responding to a horn.

The sash I raised and looked about
to see who made the noise.
"Your cows are out! Your cows are out!"
exclaimed a frantic voice.

I quickly found my underwear,
my pants, and then my shirt.
I told my wife, "Don't worry dear,
I'm sure I won't get hurt."

I flew downstairs, put on my boots
and hurried out the door.
My Grandson's car had made the toots
that woke me up before.

His wife and he had stopped the herd
from heading for the road.

But then the bull, whose ire was stirred,
was in a fighting mode.

He didn't want to go back through
the gate where they escaped.
I talked to him and told him to
behave, but he just gaped

at me and shook his big old head
as if to say, "I'm tough!
Leave me alone, go back to bed,
don't get in such a huff."

I thought about the danger then,
in dark 'twas hard to see.
But I just yelled at him again
to "get away from me.

Go back in there where you belong."
I ran at him and waved.
If I just had a pitchfork prong
I'd sure make him behave.

But suddenly he turned around,
ran through the open gate,
back in the field without a sound,
although he was irate.

He took his herd, went out of sight,
they melted in the black.
I fixed the broken latch that night
then crawled back in the sack.

I'm thankful that my grandkids cared
to stop and give a toot,
then help me, though a little scared,
to put them in "to boot."

The words a farmer thinks about
and hopes he never hears,
"The cows are out! The cows are out!"
are of his greatest fears.

THE MEDICARE BAND

I sang and played piano and banjo uke for this group in Bay city, Texas. Making the "old folks" in the nursing home happy, made us happy. Most of us were in our 70's. This poem was awarded 5th place internationally at Montgomery, AL. in 2007.

We set up microphones for six;
one had a music stand.
Our members were a motley mix,
known as The Medicare Band.
Our songs, as old as we, and more,
would fall on ears of age.
They had heard these songs before;
no need for book or page.
The wheel-chairs gathered 'round the room,
the nurses helped them park.
To take away the practiced gloom
were those whose nature sparked.
We sang and played the violins,
the banjo, harp, guitars.
When we were through, applause and grins
would tell us we were stars.
"You made me feel so happy
when you sang for us today.
If it was slow or snappy
I just loved it any way."
So said a voice so cheery
as she reached out for my hand.
Her shining eyes were teary

like she'd been in Wonderland.
I took her hand; we talked a bit,
about her fav'rite song.
My hand, she held tight, wouldn't quit,
but I had to move along.
Here came more wheel-chairs moving slow,
they formed a crooked line.
I sensed they wouldn't let me go
without their hand in mine.
When I conversed with one of them,
the others' courage rose.
They saw that I would not condemn
defects they might disclose.

They reached for love to get, and give
by clinging to my hand,
to show their hope that they could live,
and complement our band.
Most everyone had crippled arms
or legs, or twisted feet.
In younger days with grace and charms
they danced to any beat.
But now, songs they had memorized
were still deep down inside.
When hearing as we harmonized
left many misty-eyed.

"Oh, thank you sir", I heard one say,
"my mouth framed every word.
Those memories you stirred today
were sweet—so glad I heard."
Though some were ill and couldn't speak,
their eyes said loving things.
Their hands, though frail, and sometimes weak,
disclosed a heart that sings.

Our hearts were touched, emotions welled,
we shed a tear or two.
The smiles prevailed, gloom was dispelled,
it warmed us through and through.
An hour from our busy day
was not a sacrifice.
The love we shared, I have to say,
was warm, was good, was nice.

THE SIMPLE PRAYER

"Seek and ye shall find."

We do not need trumpets or edicts from kings
to open the heavens above.
We don't need an earth quake, or other harsh things
to know with a sureness, His love.
We know all it takes is a prayer of the meek,
in humbleness, earnestness, said,
to open the heavens, inspire as we seek,
and are filled with His life giving bread.

THE TEST

Written on 10/29/05, this Hsinku poem placed 5th internationally for the World Congress of Poets 2007.

I studied hard, the test was long,
I thought I knew the subject well.
I answered questions, some were wrong,
the test was life. Lord, save me from Hell!

CYCLES OF WAR

I wrote this for the Hsinku poetry contest in Tai'an, China in October 2005, sponsored by the World Congress of Poets. It won 4th place internationally.

A nation in poverty from war turns to God.
Poverty is quelled, blessings increase.
Power and greed and wars quickly grow.
Wealth is the bane of peace.

EXCUSE? LIVE ON STAGE

I wrote this to counter my bent to give excuses. Written 1/26/01 I chastised myself, then revised it in 2010 to clarify my chastisement with greater power.

Why an excuse? To save face we act out
an apologetic alibi of
justification for our faults.
Fear also becomes a possible
instigator of excuse as it sets
the stage of our minds with other

props such as pride, greed, and
the plaudits of man. The tainted
curtain rises as we conjure up the

power of deceitful thoughts to
achieve an end, complimentary to our
own self righteousness. Fear of failure

also assists the development of exaggeration
and becomes the prompter from behind
the curtain when reality will not

abridge deceit in its attempt to meld
into truth. When the final scene
is over there is no power or reward
in an excuse.

A DOG NAMED BOB

This was written in March, 2009, while thinking of and blessing my mother for her grit and determination. It also brought to my mind our wonderful old dog, Bob.

When a farmer is working hard, heavy in debt,
he looks for those shortcuts to help him, and yet,
he must choose them carefully; he must not fail,
especially if it takes milk from his pail.
A dairyman's hours are never enough!
Rising early, late to bed, can be pretty rough.
We Valentine boys had an unusual dad,
tough and dependable, he was ironclad
in his will to succeed at all costs it did seem.
His animals loved him, his dog, cows and team.
When old Rover died, Dad found a "new" dog;
a surprise that it came not from Sears catalog.
His name was just "Bob," so timid he was,
for he had been beaten so hard without cause
by his former owner, he cowered and crawled
if Dad raised his voice anytime that he called
him or pointed his finger at him scoldingly.
Bob was too sensitive and shy, we could see.
It took several months of kindness and love
and romping and playing that he rose above
the fear of a whipping, tongue lashing or worse.
Old Bob had to conquer a crippling curse.
He had a shepherding instinct for cows
and soon brought them in with his muffled bow-wows.

In a black early morn and cows in the field
Dad would send him alone, though the cows were concealed
by the dark, he would start them to come to the barn.
If they didn't hurry he would bark just to warn,
then nip at their heels and chase them away.
Then Dad would say, "Easy, Bob," give him some praise,
and send him on back if he missed any strays.
Bob was a "shortcut" that saved Dad much time.
Just saying his name would make the cows mind.
Our farm was divided by the Wynooche River.
The water was cold enough; made us all shiver.
But Bob had long hair, and he loved to swim.
With cows on the other side we would send him
to comb through the brush and chase them across.
They hurried to heed him, for he was their boss.

One day, a farmer who, five miles away,
called up my mother to rudely convey
that some cattle of ours had got in his field
and she better get them out. He wouldn't yield,
he'd call in the law if she didn't come then.
Mother was frantic and told him her plight,
begged him to wait 'til her men came that night,
for Dad was away and we kids were in school,
and she, eight months pregnant, but that orn'ry fool
didn't care. Mom put Bob in the trunk of her car.
When she arrived she thought it bizarre
the man wouldn't help her drive our cattle out.
She let out old Bob and he went round about
and soon had them on the road to our place.
Mother and Bob's five mile cattle chase
was a success. The orn'ry old farmer was known
after that as a cad, a poor neighbor, a drone.
But Bob saved the day, a hero was he
to my mother and dad and my brother and me.

ABOUT CONAN

Conan Baxter, one of my 28 grandsons, was deathly ill when just about a year old. I wrote this on Dec. 30, 2004 after giving him a healing blessing. He recovered fully.

Little fingers, pink and gripping as they surround my index finger, grasping desperately, as if to draw strength into his perfect little body, gasping for the air, that precious life-giving air he needs to maintain mortal life. He opens his big expressive, beautiful eyes and looks at me questioningly, but with perfect faith that he will be able to overcome the feverish sickness that threatens to strangle him. A little smile crosses his face as he recognizes his grandpa, who has grown to love him dearly. That precious little child, that wonderful gift from our Heavenly Father, who, with help and nurturing from his loving parents, grandparents, and far extended family will overcome the death that tries to trap him and limit him to one short year of earthly existence. He has great works to perform as a valiant man of God.

DEFY ENMITY

Written Jan.3, 2003, it was clear to me that we must not allow enmity or hostility to infect us. It truly is Satan's tool.

Enmity toward God and fellowmen
will bring us pain, as it is Satan's tool.
The sin of pride that rolls from tongue and pen
may signify its author is a fool,
if hatred or hostility, therein,
will quash the good, and bitterness enhance.
Then man will play old Satan's song of sin,
while those around him join with savage dance.

The antidote is found if men repent,
proceeding with a broken, contrite heart.
That enmity will weaken 'til it's spent
and join the trash of which it is a part.
Humility and love can take its place;
obedience and meekness fill the void
till enmity and pride He will erase.
Then God and man are ever overjoyed.

WHERE IS PEACE?

Written 12/27/07, the question seems to have no answer.

The wonders of the universe are constantly evolving,
the changes of the changes never cease.
Though man continues study and is ever problem solving,
the problem no one solves is "Where is peace?"

CROSBY'S SLAUGHTERHOUSE

This poem fills in another part of Crosby Valentine's legacy as a farmer in the upper Wynooche Valley. Written in Feb. 2009, the old structure still stands on the Wheeler Road farm but is disintegrating.

A tireless Crosby Valentine was always on the run.
A beef and dairy farmer with a cleaver, knife, and gun;
he trained himself to butcher beef; had used a storage shed,
but beef demand dictated that he kills a lot more head.
He hired old Tony Reinkins with his concrete mixing skill
to build a good foundation for a slaughterhouse, to kill
and hang as much as seven beef and sev'ral fattened veal.
The carpenter who worked with Valentine was "such a deal."

His name was Samuel Crass, who never charged what he was worth.
A quiet gentle man was he, soft-spoken, down to earth.
Oh, Sam knew how to build and Crosby drew him his design,
for Crosby worked in other shops and butchered beef and swine.
He worked in Hoquiam for Buzz Sharp, and Hensler's Brady Shop.
Designed the slaughterhouse he built from bottom to the top.
He knew just what would work the best… efficiency was prime.
For, he was busy with his farm, with little extra time.

Some walls were filled with sawdust so the meat could hang and cool.
Refrigeration, there was none, but cleanliness, the rule.
A strong corral constructed of some heavy posts and rails,
adjoined the handy slaughterhouse to act as cattle jails.
The blood and fluids from the beef drained o'er the river bank,
to mix with water flowing there that no one ever drank.
The fish, however, liked the stuff and came from far and near,
to line up there on slaughter days, like having Christmas cheer.

One thing was very evident, the fish got big and fat.
(The government would frown these days; those days were not like that)

The aging, graying slaughterhouse is not used anymore.
Though seasons come and seasons go, no beef roll out its door.
It served a special purpose in a time when war was on.
And all the young men from the farms were drafted and were gone.

Crosby bought his neighbor's cattle if they were for sale;
their steers and bulls, their dairy cows whose milk wouldn't fill a pail.
Meat was scarce and butcher shops in towns had empty cases.
Crosby sold his beef around, brought smiles to many faces.

That slaughterhouse, its mission filled, is starting to decay.
The place where there were many deaths is dying fast away.
It seems appropriate to me, the cycle you can trust.
Whatever things are made to be, they end up "dust to dust."

REMARKABLE NONSENSE
SONNET #32

You won't learn anything from this poem. It sorts of represents the world, written 6/5/08, it placed 4th in the free verse category, although it is a sonnet.

Where are we, anyhow,
past, or future, in the now?
Where is time before it's spent?
Do we wonder where it went?

How long ago was just before?
When do we start to gain rapport?
Just how early is too soon?
When do notes become a tune?

Maybe might be definite
if it would measure by the foot.
How far up is almost full?
Can you not see when under wool?

How much is a little bit?
I can't stand more! This is it!

THERE WILL BE A BRIGHTER DAY

Written on April 2005, I published this as a memorial hymn and sang it for several funerals and memorial services. It is published in "Sing the Songs of Redeeming Love", a gospel song book by Rex B. Valentine.

There will be a brighter day.
Your loved one is just a cloud away.
The sorrow that you feel
in your heart is very real,
but the Lord will hear you when you pray.
So, look to the light
for His comfort in the night,
the pain and the doubts will fade away.
Your vision may be dim,
but if you follow Him,
There Will Be a Brighter Day.

When your loved one slips away,
remember (he) she is on the Lords high way.
The journey is not far,
just beyond a shining star
and (he) she will find a brighter day.

Our time on earth is short,
to Him we must report.
We come to the end of our stay.
The Lord is over all
and when we hear his call,
There Will Be a Brighter Day.

Our temple here is made of clay.
Without our spirit life it will decay.
But we will travel on
through His light and love 'til dawn;
for the Lord will lead us on our way.

So, look to the light
for His comfort in the night;
the pain and the doubts will fade away.
Our vision may be dim,
but if we follow Him,
There Will Be a Brighter Day.

THOSE DIRTY SWIMMERS
VILLANELLE #10

Written at Mazatlan, Mexico after attempting to swim in a pool, May 2005, I stretched it a little.

I can't believe what happens at the pool
each time I go to have a private swim.
It seems that all the swimmers there are cruel.

I read the signs and follow every rule
And though my chance for trouble should be slim,
I can't believe what happens at the pool.

I slip into the water, it's so cool.
Then someone hits me diving from the rim.
It seems that all the swimmers there are cruel.

I yell at him, he yells at me "you fool,
Go get your clothes and go back to the gym."
I can't believe what happens at the pool.

I try to swim when kids are still in school
'cause splashes in my eyes make vision dim.
It seems that all the swimmers there are cruel.

They snap me with their towels, a vicious tool
and push me under water at a whim.
I can't believe what happens at the pool.
It seems that all the swimmers there are cruel.

TWENTY SEASONS IN A YEAR?

Written on our Texas mission in June of 2006. Women's habits when buying clothes and shoes can make men wince.

Though female styles of clothes and shoes do change,
some women are misguided in their thoughts.
They seem to think their duds must be exchanged
each time they see a store where clothes they've bought.
It is a wonder they can keep a track
of everything they buy, or presents get,
but they know where and when to take them back,
to trade them in with gladness, not regret.

There seems to be no norm to be in style,
for styles change each time they go to town.
They wear an outfit once, and then they smile,

and Goodwill gets a blouse, or pants, or gown.

Variety, the spice of life, they say,
is evident when some of them buy shoes.
They must have different styles every day,
so many colors it is hard to choose.

One alibi is they "must be in season".
Each color for a certain time of year.
But if they're North or South there is no reason
for twenty seasons in a hemisphere.

Oh well, we men can take it in our strides.
We like to see them beautiful and fine.
We loved them when they were our needy brides,
and love them now. And that's the bottom line.

UNFORGETTABLE SEVENTY-FIFTH BIRTHDAY

It was a great party held 2/7/09, I loved it.

It's hard to remember how forgetful I am,
I turned seventy-five today.
When I see my old friends, it's a "guess who" program,
I don't know them so they "go away."
I used to recall everybody I saw,
Their names would just pop in my head.
But now all I think is, he's someone's grandpa,
I'm surprised, 'cause I thought he was dead.
I tie a white string on my finger at times
to remember our groceries are low.
When I get to town, I don't have a dime
'cause my wallet with me didn't go.

Oh what shall I do? My mem'ry's so bad.
I call all my kids the wrong names.
When they come home it makes them feel sad
that I'm playing these memory games.
So I'll practice each day, I'll jack up my brain
and inject it with brilliant recall,
Then when I'm eighty I won't have to strain,
I'll forget that I worried at all.

WHO WERE THOSE WHO KEPT THE FAITH?

This poem was written in March 1997 to be used on Church Pioneer Day July 23rd. It tells the story of the Mormon Migration west from Illinois to Utah in wagons and handcarts.

Jesus built His church by those receiving revelation.
Revelation was the Rock; the church's true foundation.
The Saints of God were following the Spirit of the Lord,
that guided them from day to day, His blessings to afford.

Man had learned to follow man while ages dark had ruled;
then God's church returned to earth; by prophet's men were schooled.
The persecutors of the Saints, for giving prophets heed,
had burned their homes, their barns, their crops; and left them all in need.
Prophets of the Lord could see a land of beauty fair;
visions of a place of peace for those who'd journey there.
The way was long, the trail so rough, the weather hot or cold.
But Pioneers with faith would go wherever they were told.
Who were those who kept the faith in God and in His leaders?
Who were those who 'round the campfire listened to His readers?
Courageous souls of simple faith who walked or rode or shoved
to reach a place where they could follow Christ, the One they loved.
Wagons rolled and handcarts creaked along through mud and dust.
Weary pilgrims sang their songs of courage and of trust.

The restoration of His gospel strong within their hearts
renewed their energy to drive their wagons, pull their carts.

There were those they left along the trail, those dearest ones.
Some were old, and some were frail; their daughters and their sons,
whose lives were sacrificed to reach the unknown Promised Land.
But faith was strong they'd meet again through God's Eternal Plan.
We, too, must be pioneers who follow God's commands.
Leaders who will serve our fellow man with helping hands;
with hearts so true and faithful we will never go astray,
no matter what the pressures are, we'll walk the narrow way;

knowing that the sacrifices we'll be asked to make
may be very hard for us—out lives may be at stake.
We hope our strength and courage will be as the pioneers
who listened to the prophets of the Lord in former years.
Who were those who kept the faith? The answer should be clear.
Those of olden times, the martyrs and the pioneers,
and every soul who doesn't deviate from truth and right,
but keeps the faith in Jesus Christ and lives within His light.

SOW WITH LOVE
VILLANELLE #14

I wrote this Villanelle poem 6/19/07 while on a trip through Mississippi with Diane. I was thinking about helping others.

I hope that you will plant this seed
and watch your garden grow.
Your satisfaction's guaranteed

providing you cut any weed
the minute it should show.
I hope that you will plant this seed.

Directions on the package, heed,
and don't forget to hoe;
your satisfaction's guaranteed.

Your hungry neighbors have a need
a little extra, sow
I hope that you will plant this seed

for it will be a kindly deed,
to share your food with them, you know.
Your satisfaction's guaranteed.

The good you do will more than feed,
you'll bless them when they're feeling low.
I hope that you will plant this seed;
your satisfaction's guaranteed.

WISDOM

Written 9/4/10, as I was contemplating my progress toward wisdom

Wisdom has no special season;
nor does it need any style.
Still, if it's enhanced by reason,
will not hurt or foster guile.

Wisdom has a feel for timing,
knowing when to stop or go,
binding ego's bent for climbing,
curbing one's desire to show.

Wisdom loves consideration,
knowing when to get or give,
basking in anticipation
of each person's joy to live.

THE BEACH VENDORS OF MEXICO

This was written after spending time on the beach at Mazatlan, Mexico. Though a distraction at times, I admired their dedication to their sales work.

The beaches in Mexico are no place to send her
if she has some money to spend.
While sitting and sunning there's many a vendor
who's waving his wares like a friend.

There're puppets that jiggle and dance on the sand,
dark glasses and hats of all kinds.
Jewelry for ears, necks, or wrists, or your hand,
and scarves for your head or behind.

Fruit dishes balanced on heads in flat trays,
an assortment to tickle your taste.
Trinkets and carvings, bright colored displays
to tie on your arms or your waist.

None of them stutter when calling to you;
they're brave and they're bold and they're brash.
They whistle or wave when they come into view,
looking for buyers with cash.
They bargain and haggle to get you to buy.
Their prices keep coming on down,
but when they reach bottom they moan and they cry,
make pitiful faces and sounds.

They finish with stories of how they're so poor,
or say they have nothing to eat;
or going to school, or a dozen things more,
or their kids need some shoes for their feet.

Still, down under all they are people, like us.
And we all should admire them for grit.
They stay on the job with a minimum of fuss,

while hefting their goods or their kit,
standing and walking all day on the sands,
the boiling hot sun on their backs.
I'm sure they get tired. Life's heavy demands
are more than their packs and their sacks.

Some of us soften, succumb to their wiles,
then brag of our bargains and buys;
remembering faces that broke into smiles
from success after dozens of tries.

OBSERVATIONS OF A POET

Written on October 15, 2006, after mission for the church in Texas where I wrote many poems and some music.

With poetry, one can write a whole chapter in one line;
especially if there is love between the words.
The fun of reminiscing is greatly heightened
when participants remember and compare common experiences.
Dreams become real when later shared with a friend.
One can fill in the blank spaces and leap from a sketchy scene
to one that is vivid, by building one's own bridges
on the spot with new-born facts.
Many times goals can be reached without negatives
if one overlooks the "what-ifs".
Doubts may be removed or cancelled out
by euphoric X's in enthusiastic boxes.

GIVING

A wonderful trait! Inspired Jan., 9, 2003 by the thankfulness in my heart.

Giving is a part of life that has no bounds.
There is no required beginning or end, no squares or rounds
to fill, no measurement or quota, but giving can run free
as a stream fed from springs whose source one cannot see.

Giving may be inspired by a spirit deep within us, also unseen.
It can be spontaneous as the rain from a passing cloud,
or planned for hours, days, months, or years.
It can cause laughter, joy-fullness, gratitude or tears.

Gifts can be that which we don't need,
our surplus, or gifts can be a share of that which we receive.
Then, gifts can also be from the compassion of our very souls,
possibly at great sacrifice.
So was the gift of God's only begotten Son, Jesus Christ,
the greatest gift mankind has ever known.

STUCK WITH STICKS

I wrote this after waking up from surgery on my right knee on 2/19/04, anxious to dispatch my crutches.

The woozy world of anesthetics
does <u>not</u> include robust athletics...
As I regain my consciousness
I notice retained paunchiness.
I haven't lost a lot of fat
for this is this and that is that.
Instead of running out to play
they say I'll have to wait a day.

The knee they expertly repaired
was fixed by one who really cared.

But I can't run, or climb, or jump;
instead there is a crutches thump.

So I will race another day
when I have thrown those sticks away.

OPEN DOORS

New experiences and unknown places always have intrigued me. I've been a curious adventurer, but I've already decided what I'll do under certain circumstances to protect me, and mine, from harm.

Nothing much intrigues me more
than coming to an open door.
I'm curious of anything
a newly opened door can bring,
especially if it's a-jar
and I can't see in very far.
I wonder what the circumstance
could be? Coincidental chance
I came along in time to see
that door unlatched and calling me?
Should I step through that open door?
I've never been in there before.
Or should I quell this strong desire
and stop myself, not play with fire?
What is the source that pressures me,
that plays my curiosity?
A wind of ill, or Heaven sent?
What causes this predicament?

I know I've trod this road before.
My soul within, my spirit core
has published truth, directions sure,
to guide with revelation pure.
Decisions I have made before
I ever saw that open door.
So I will reach into my mind;
the answers there I predesigned.
And will not worry anymore.
I'll pass, or take an open door.

PRECIOUS WATER
VILIANELLE #7

Written 11/9/04 to express the fact that dreams do not always share reality.

Oh, for a drink of water in a glass.
Just water wet and sweet of any brand
from any lake or stream or cool crevasse.

Its value precious, jewels cannot surpass.
When thirst was king; no water was at hand.
Oh, for a drink of water in a glass.

My throat was dry. I'd walked o'er sand and grass,
no water to be had in that dry land
from any lake or stream or cool crevasse.

I staggered 'neath the boiling sun, alas,
mirages fooled me, I could hardly stand.
Oh, for a drink of water in a glass.

I saw a lake so big I could not pass.
But when I reached its shore 'twas rippling sand.
Not any lake or stream or cool crevasse.

Then I awoke! My airplane seat, first class!
The steward said, "I'm here at your command."
"Oh, please, a drink of water in a glass
from any lake or stream or cool crevasse?"

DISCIPLINE AND LOVE CONQUERS SELF

Written on Nov. 6, 2009, it describes some of my life's progress, and dad's role.

Many were the lessons learned
when farming with my Dad.
He taught, that privilege was earned,
while I a little lad.

Dad taught me how to do my chores
on time and with a smile.
He showed much love and gave encores
when I'd surmount a trial.

Still, he could be demanding, too,
would push me to succeed.
He gave me more than I could do
at times, then intercede
and help me finish up my task
when he could see my need.

He didn't like it when I'd ask
if orders he'd repeat.
He wanted me to hear them once,
and do the job complete.

It seems as if he didn't know
I was a different kind.
I wasn't physical and so
did exercise my mind.

But he would bring me down to earth
with a pitchfork in my hand,
and teach me I had double worth
when labor I could stand.

His love of sports infected me;
I hardened as I grew.
He sacrificed great hours to see
I caught a ball and threw.

While milking cows by hand we'd sing,
and practice mental math.
Then I'd hear more than cow bells ring
while on that learning path.

He forced me to exceed my norm,
in stamina and strength.
Till I enjoyed and could perform
hard tasks at any length.

And then one day I left my home
and Daddy's strong demands.
It wasn't long till I had come
to thank him for strong stands.

But there was much for me to learn,
to create with my mind,
to write, to plan, to love, discern,
what God would have me find.

The combination of the things
my Dad instilled in me,
along with nature's song that sings
a constant melody,

has let me live a verdant life,
productive to the max,
a family, a lovely wife,
a time where nothing lacks.

DAD'S DIRTY RAG

This was written May 22, 2010 at Brother Randy and his wife Carol's request so we would always remember the discipline that encouraged us to be better boys.

In looking back, I must say Dad was usually clean.
While working hard he often broke a sweat.
Farm work was physical, but he had good hygiene.
Perspiration freely bathed his face, and wet-
ness dripped off the end of his nose, but it had no smell.
Dad had been taught to enjoy hard labor. His spirit
and his body seemed to be cleansed, we could tell,
while we boys could see a tough job and fear it.
Sometimes we thought our Dad was a little mean
when we failed to please him with our work, or lack of.
His instructions usually were detailed, easy seen,
but if we shirked our duties he used some "tough love".
A spanking in the wood-shed with a split shake
brought real physical pain, as did a swat with Uncle Kenneth's belt.
But we rarely did anything bad enough to make
him resort to those stinging blows we really felt.
We have since agreed, that the punishment dreaded most
was to be swatted around the neck with Dad's Dirty Rag.
It was cut from a burlap sack when a mouse had chewed a hole,
so it wouldn't hold the grain and became a leaky bag.
That rough burlap rag was about one foot and a half square.
When he milked a cow by hand he draped it over his knee.
He used the thing to wipe the udder clean. He'd then prepare
to squirt the milk into the open pail, and if by chance he'd see
some dirt or "other stuff" he'd wipe it off with the rag.
When he finished milking that cow, he'd drape the rag over his milking stool
and take the milk to the milk house.
When back, he'd wipe off the next cow's bag
with his trusty rag. If her teats were sore, it was the rule
to apply some Watkins's salve and work it in with a "clean"
corner of the rag. This allowed the milking to continue
without hurting the cow. Consequently, the rag was never seen

to be really clean, except when he would make one that was new.
The dirty rag discipline seldom was used
on Randy or me, for we tried hard to please.
Still, Dad had a temper and it was short fused.
In mornings if we overslept, warm or freeze,
he'd storm in the house and he'd yell for us boys.
To get to the barn fast, and by him we'd rush,
for when the screen door slammed it made enough noise,
that we woke up running, our red faces flushed.
When we swished by him we tried hard to duck
'cause that foul smelling rag would wrap 'round our necks.
We knew if he missed us, it would be pure luck,
but we never were fired or missed our paychecks.

JUST WAITING

For that special one, written August 2002 on the way home.

At the airport...
waiting, waiting...
for a plane?...Yes, and
no. The plane will
come and I'll still be
waiting. Waiting to
start home? Yes, and
no. We will start home
and I'll still be waiting.
Waiting to touch down?
Yes, and no. We'll touch
down and I'll still be
waiting. Waiting to touch
<u>you</u>? <u>Yes</u>, waiting to
touch <u>you</u>.

DEAR AUNTIE IS OLDER
VILLANELLE #1

My first villanelle, written on Feb., 1998, after taking a poetry class from Joanne Clark. It features my dear sweet Aunt Edith (Easter) Hill who never had children of her own but doted on her nieces and nephews. She died a few years later and this tribute was read at her funeral.

She was always so loving to me;
though married, no child of her own.
Dear Auntie is older and soon will be free.

Dresses and dolls for her nieces with glee
she would sew, up all night all alone.
She was always so loving to me.

Coats for her nephews, how lucky were we,
they were perfectly fitted and sewn.
Dear Auntie is older and soon will be free.

Who was her favorite? I thought it was me.
But I wonder, now that I'm grown.
She was always so loving to me.

It seems that each niece thought it was she.
Each nephew thought he her gemstone.
Dear Auntie is older and soon will be free.

Now she is older! There's no rivalry,
her feebleness we will enthrone.
She was always so loving to me.
Dear Auntie is older and soon will be free.

FINDING HAPPINESS IN LIFE
SONNET #29

Written on vacation while waiting to fly and flying to Maui to be with my daughter Kerry Petersen and family.

What fun it is when we are of an age
that everything is so exciting, new!
Why, we can hardly wait to turn a page,
or play a game, or television view.

Then music, sports, and studies form the text
that raises pulse and competition drives.
The most exciting thing of all comes next;
the other sex may captivate our lives.

This leads to marriage with that special one,
the sharing of two souls, in sorrow, joy,
then new vocations, always on the run,
the greatest thrill, a new-born girl or boy!

The fun of any age depends on fire
emitting from within, known as DESIRE.

MY GARAGE, TOO SMALL?

These toys, trikes, bikes, and scooters, are known as Grandpa and Grandma's fleet. With a new four-foot walkway around the entire house, the traffic is quite heavy at times. What a joy to me are our grandkids.

When in my own garage I drive my car
and witness in my way a bunch of toys,
(the door won't shut, I'm not in very far),

for if I smash a trike, some little boys
would weep and tell their Moms of Grandpa's sin.
Their little hearts would break, they couldn't cope.
I'm happy that my car will not go in
the garage, for it has been my dream, my hope,
to see my many grandkids coming 'round,
their fleet of wagons, trikes and bikes and cars
awaiting their return. I hear the sound
of motors revving up like string guitars,
when they a-light and rush to get their pick.
They bolt out through the door and 'round they drive
the spacious asphalt apron. They are quick.
They learn the rules of road, of life, and strive
to be the fastest or the best to share
with smaller cousins with no drive permit.
It pleases me to see them playing there.
And yes, I'm glad my car into my garage won't fit.

THE WORLD OF FORGETTORY

Our subconscious mind sticks with a problem, while our conscious mind goes blithely along, doing new things. Our power returns when they come together again. Written in Idaho while visiting daughter Annie and her husband Jason Nov. 16, 2001.

Oh the quiet world of forgettory
does masquerade as peace
when it invades our imagination.
While we are constructing the wish-it-were world
with and in our conscious minds,
so as to blot out the so-called unpleasantness of work,
responsibility, productivity and physical strain,
pretending not to remember their effects,
both good and bad, on our inner being,
our subconscious is battered and bloodied

as it tries to overcome its nakedness
while fighting life's battles alone.
Its advance scouts have fallen,
its roadmaps disintegrating
with the wetness of tears not allowed to fall,
its armor and shields too heavy to carry
and its paradigms exposed like a building
whose facade has been stricken from its face.

Oh, this quiet world of forgettory
can remove us from painful situations of real life,
but it can injure the inner mind
if it is not constructed with the guidance of prayer,
meditation, and openness to the healing light
that streams from the consciousness of a loving Father.
This light must be allowed to fill the fissures,
crevices, and hollows and bring about
the much needed healing peace
as it medicates the open wounds, left
when our conscious mind moves on ahead
to establish new experiences of planned action,
or utopian surroundings.
The salve of faith and love joins the situation of hope
as the world of forgettory fades and becomes real
and our minds are rejoined to become whole again
capable of functioning in synergetic power and perfection.

LOVE IS A ROAD

Love's connection is sure. I've seen the road.

Love is a road that stretches
from you to me.
There are no times to stop or start.

It reaches from heart to heart.
This road can be traveled day and night.
There are no bends to obstruct our sight.
It's open and clear, the way is free
as it spans the space from you to me.
I take this road when around me is fear,
for it's high and safe,
the end always near.
There are no holes or hills that I can't climb.
Though I'm fast or slow
I get there on time.

THE VALENTINE ADVENTURE

I wrote this poem for my loving sweetheart, Diane Valentine on 2/14/08.

We were so poor when we began
to see ourselves as woman and man.
The phone calls and the precious hours
when talk was fresh as rain-splashed flowers.
The fun, the love, and then the laughter,
recipes for life thereafter.
You were so young and thought me wise,
an older man, who could advise
you, as you met the wiley world,
adventures only at you hurled
if you should choose to stick with me,
a curious adventure.
And now as many years have passed
you're still expecting first and last
the unknown tricks of Father Time
to touch your life and make it rhyme
with me, my love, because you're mine,
a tried and loving Valentine.

EXPECTATION
SONNET #17

This describes my feelings for my 42 grandchildren, each one so unique, written I 2009.

The grandchild worms his way into your heart,
at first, by chance, evading loving gaze.
Then smiles begin that make you feel a part
of his development, then words, a phrase.
By then you hang on every utterance.
There can't be any other one so smart!
Intelligence just isn't there by chance;
his pedigree says you gave him his start.

And when he learns his ABC's and counts,
you frequently encourage him, repeat,
until his confidence, in time, surmounts
a threshold that is bordering conceit.

What a wonder! He's magnificent, a joy!
Though average, he's the best! He's Grandpa's boy.

THE BENEFACTORS OF GOD'S SPIRIT AND LOVE

Written in 3/2003 this poem expresses the greatest power that I felt, as it affected my life and still affects it.

Oh, Great God; Thy subtle, sublime Spirit
speaks so softly, yet so powerfully, that
even the trees hear Thee. They acknowledge Thy
love as their branches bow beautifully before

Thee, while the gentle breeze stimulates their adoring replies.
The antennae of even the smallest insects receives
Thy instructions of where to find food and shelter, and warns them
of approaching dangers.
The rocks break from the vibrations of Thy voice
when they hear Thy commands and move monstrous mountains.
All fish and other creatures of the sea are tuned
to Thy wavelengths. They happily obey Thy will
without knowing why, as the cycles of life ebb and flow.
Thy sweet spirit carries over,
through and across the great and small bodies of water continually.

All animals are tuned to Thy sixth sense, that
somehow seems to show them, glimpses of the
future; warning them or enticing them to move,
hide, lie still, observe, or run, to preserve life
as they know it, or submit to the closing acts
of their life's stage.

Man has not been left out or slighted. He is a
spirit being in a physical world, which tries to
quench the Spirit within him. Satan's grasp is repelled
by angels that function best when man yields his
spirit to their care, allowing Thee, Oh Great God, through them
to direct his paths with foresight, hindsight, and
vision of the now. Man, though is free to choose
good or evil. He has great protection if he chooses good.

The inspiration of God may, at man's volition, entwine
with man's spirit. The synergetic power produced
therewith makes man the greatest benefactor of
God's spirit and love. Therefore, the secrets and mysteries
of the universe will continually be unlocked
and stored for future generations by and
through the miracles of computer science.

When man embraces peace, love flourishes, which is
the great single well-spring of power for all creation.
Oh Great God, teach us unconditional love through thy Spirit,
that we may know and promote peace on earth. Amen

SHOPPING CRISIS

Written while waiting in a Texas shopping mall for my wife, and observing some unfortunate shoppers (not my beautiful wife). 9/23/05

A woman shopping for new slacks
can be affected by BIG MACS.

When she realizes what her size is,
it can cause a shopping crisis.

A time before she wore a "ten,"
but this is now, and that was then.

MY SPIRIT

Our spirits do wonderful things to and for us if we allow our God to direct our thoughts so we can eventually live with him again.

My spirit rides before me
on wings of silent power
one cannot see
grappling with worldly pressures.

I fly protected skies
no rudder do I need
I navigate by stars
without a compass. From life's frictions
I leave a trail of sparks
whose melting flashes dim
as time and space slowly devours them.
I suffer just flesh wounds of no vital consequences
to me on my directed journey.
My spirit rides ahead like a blocker
in a football game, clearing the way of
those who would stop or impede me,
hurt me or keep me from my goals.

My spirit knows which way I will run,
how I dodge to escape the devilish
meanness of man's lower form, and
man's greediness lodged in the minds
of "successful" upper-classers.
Even my sleep is directed by my spirit
if I use my waking hours to praise
my Maker and give thanks for all
things great and small, good or bad.
Dreams may soothe my battered mind
with healing. In them I fly
unimpeded without wings.
Levitation is mine at my directed will.
My spirit lifts me, protects me,
converses with me, consoles me,
as it entwines with the Spirit All
Powerful, to lead me home again.

DESSERT----MY GREATEST PLEASURE

This poem was entered in the State Grange contest with a desert theme, in April, 2009 and received a blue ribbon.

Eating is my favorite sport
and now I'll give a full report.

Beans and tatters sure taste good!
I eat my carrots like I should.

I like chicken, beef and pork
and eat them with a knife and fork.

But when I get to my dessert,
I don't wait or plan, or flirt.

A knife, or fork, or spoon will do,
or I might use my fingers too.

Dessert inspires poetic vibes,
my greatest pleasure it describes.

THERE IS POWER IN THE FAST
VILLANELLE #8

Our family believes that denying food for a day or more gives us spiritual power when used with fervent prayer for others in need.

There is great power in the fast
The Lord did show us all, the way.
It's for the now as in the past.

Obtain that strength our Father hast
and be a blessing in our day.
There is great power in the fast.

Begin with prayer, petitions cast
to Heavn'ly Father as you may.
It's for the now as in the past.

It may be, you will be aghast
with inspiration as you pray,
(There is great power in the fast.)

for God's potential love is vast,
and angels act without delay.
It's for the now as in the past.

It matters not if first or last,
the Spirit never goes astray.
There is great power in the fast.
it's for the now, as in the past.

DOUBLE TALK, DOUBLE RHYME, SPIRIT ANSWER

I started this poem in 2006, finished and revised it in April of 2009. It describes our mixed up world.

The mysteries of life are so intriguing
that everywhere "wise men" keep searching and digging.
The answers they find are inspiring more questions
that cultivate minds to make wilder suggestions.

They say that big is smaller, short is taller;
that when you holler, there is not a caller.

Their universe is shrinking while it's growing,
which keeps the smart ones thinking, never knowing.

The world, by their advice, is less today
as oceans grow from ice that melts away.
There are those who tell us black is white,
and they are zealous proving wrong is right.

They fight to show that war will bring in peace,
make rich so poor, that goodness will increase.
In retrospect they speak of great success
but leave a world that's bleak and in a mess.

Enlightenment will land upon a few.
The rest won't understand, their minds askew.
The Maker of all things made no mistakes,
from riches sought by kings to lowly snakes.

Now, blindness is a fault of natural man,
who savors not the salt of Heaven's Plan.
The Spirit speaks in soft, subduing sounds,
but man's mind, aloft, can't hear as he expounds.

RE-RUNS IN THE THEATRE OF LIFE

This was originally written for my mother-in-law, H. Louise (Terry) Owen and her sister, whose birthdays were both on 12/5/1901. A lovely woman, mother Owen, was 86 then. This was a tribute to their lives. The poem later won first place in the contest of the World Congress of Poets for poems of any style, at the 21st conference held in Nicaragua in 2009, and contributed to my honor of receiving the top award of Laureate Man of Letters-2009, for that organization.

Birthdays are a special time
when we recount the years.
In looking back, we view the film

of happiness and tears.
As images of childhood days
flash quickly through our minds,
like corners of the Big-Little-Books,
or a diary's passionate lines.
Sometimes we may catch a frame
so bold the projector stops.
That picture; so exciting,
oh, so beautiful! It's tops,
until it jogs our memory
of other matchless scenes
including some that never happened
in the real, just dreams.
Sometimes, though, we're brought to tears
by heartaches, failures, pain.
By visions dark, of times we
hope we'll never see again.
Those pictures, stark and sharply
framed with sorrow and despair,
we allow to fade in sunlight, bright;
we cut, we splice, repair.
Forgiveness is that splicing tape,
erasing things of wrong;
healing, patching, with the love
that's part of Heaven's song.
There are those who know that love,
they've shared it all their days.
They've patched their films with love
and goodness in their quiet ways.
They are successes in their fields
as husbands, wives and friends.
Their legacy, their families
on a reel that never ends.

GOD'S WORK MUST GO ON

We have a choice on who to follow and what to do. Oct., 14, 2006

God's work must go on and fill every void.
His word and his song be ever enjoyed.

The privilege of thought, the right to express,
to say, or say not, but always to bless.

God's work must go on; his love we proclaim
through Jesus, his Son, who death overcame.

We seek and we pray for truth to befall
upon us today, our spirits enthrall.

God's work must go on and we are his voice
to wake everyone to know of their choice

to follow the Lord and live in his light,
or live by the sword until all becomes night.

THE WATERFALL—REMEMBER?

In looking for a waterfall for a client to purchase, I experienced several beautiful ones. They impressed me so, I wrote this 4/17/06.

Have you ever heard that pelting, swishing, call
and know you're listening to a waterfall?
There's something magic about the sound,
the rushing water has no bounds.
The splash, the spray, goes everywhere
it wants to go. The misty air
will lick your face like satin lace,

refresh your lips like cotton tips
your mother used, when you were bruised,
that softest touch, your pain defused.
Yes, there is healing in that sound
that gives a feeling all around
of letting go of cares and sorrows,
daring to think of sweet tomorrows.
The waterfall drowns out the noise
of a busy world; instead, deploys
the soothing splatter
of water on rocks,
a musical chatter,
neither Mozart's nor Bach's,
just matter on matter, that really
doesn't matter.

INSPIRATION, KNOWLEDGE, WISDOM

These three traits are blessings available to all who seek. August 2002

I'm not too old to learn.
I'm not too young to know.
Of knowledge I discern
ev'n in the vertigo.

My vision does imply
the state of things to come,
though skeptics constant-try
to say my brain is numb.

Prophetic strains impart
without me knowing why.
They say I'm not that smart
and stifle my reply.

But angels 'round me stay,
to help me is their lot.
Although I sometimes stray
and cancel heav'nly thought.

The Light of Truth returns,
like dawn renews the day;
refreshes, washes. Spurns
the evil spirit's play.

The door is open wide
as knowledge fills the air.
There wisdom may abide
my mind, my soul, my prayer.

MY MIND, A MINE

We must be constantly careful what we put into our wonderful minds, and more careful of what we allow to escape.

My mind is a deposit from my Heavenly Creator
with a mother lode of gold in abundance within,
camouflaged by earthy desires and customs.

Infiltrated with passionate thoughts and feelings of "good" and "bad",
so determined by human vehicles of judgment,
my mind expands unevenly with partially filled compartments,
listing first to one side and then another
with the weight of the world and the "wait" of heaven.

I must carefully and constantly mine the gold in its purity,
expelling the dross into the slag-piles of hell,
and reject the sludge that builds up,
forming great obstacles that seek to overburden my restless spirit,
angelic impulses, and Christ like desires and directives.

There comes a time when the miner becomes Major,
providing I drop the pick and allow the sluicing waters of Heaven
to wash the impurities from the golden nuggets of my thoughts.

Then, combining my "gold mind" with my soul
I will be instantly transported to the next sphere
in a perfect form when my Creator calls.

THE BOUQUET OF LIFE

This poem is a feature poem of this book, drawing a correlation between the flowers life and the life of people. It was written for the 2001 State Grange poetry contest on March 6, 2011 and received 4th place among 405 entries.

The budding bouquet was beautiful when it arrived one day.
She put it on the windowsill, the vase which braced its stay
did complement the colors, too, the reds, the greens, the gold,
meshed with that pretty vase of blue, so lovely to behold.

Each day when she came in the room her passion for them rose.
Their beauty and their mild perfume in concert did expose
the youthful freshness of the flowers.
They were *so* alive,
that she could sense and so devour their will to live and thrive.
The buds were opening; each blossom spread into its space.
The picture made by them was awesome, it filled the pretty vase.
As time did quietly roll on there came a subtle change.
Some flowers withered, were far-gone. Those left, she rearranged.

So soon, all flowers met their end, all brilliant colors gone,
except the vase, a minuend of beauty, lingered on.
How sad it was for her to face the loss of vibrant blooms.
For now, no beauty with its grace will cheer her naked rooms.
There is a similarity, the bouquet's life and ours.

When young we reach a parity where we're as fresh as flowers.
Surroundings soon become our vase to hold us straight and true.
(Still, not everybody's place is painted pretty blue.)

But as we age, our bodies and minds do show the test of time.
We live, we love, but each one finds that final hill to climb.
Then one by one we all must fade and they must lay us by.
Like flowers, most are not afraid, we joy in life, then die.
Our earthly time is finished then; our spirits onward fly.
The flowers' seed will sprout again. We'll find new life on high.

THE MAGICAL LIBRARY

Written on Oct. 10, 2010, this memory was still clear in my mind after almost 70 years. The discovery of such an exciting home for books was new for me.

My first days of school were exciting for me;
a time I will never forget.
Miss Hunt was our teacher, a kind redhead, she;
we took turns at reading, and yet,
the words were too easy for Roland and me.
Those "Dick and Jane" stories a snap.
Each mother had started us reading at three
as we eagerly sat on her lap.
So when it was reading time, without any fuss,
Miss Hunt took our hands, 'mid odd looks.
We had no idea that she was leading us
upstairs to a room filled with books.
There were books everywhere in that wonderful land;
row upon row to extremes.
I gazed with amazement, the feeling was grand,
exceeding my thoughts and my dreams.
'Twas hard to believe my good fortune that day.
Miss Hunt turned and started to leave.

"I'll come back in an hour to get you. You stay!
You may pick any book you believe
you would like to know what its story's about,"
a magical moment for me.
Some books were too difficult; I saw without doubt.
But it thrilled me to know all were free.
Those moments took me to places unknown,
their pictures so clear and concise.
I discovered new animals, babies and grown,
Mother Goose would have thought they were nice.
Day after day we returned to that place
where the hour flew by with great speed.
Those fairy tale steps, in my mind I retrace
to the magical library to read.

SEARCH FOR THE GOLD

I try to look for the best in everyone. At times, though I forget to protect myself from harm. Written Feb., 15, 2002 while on vacation.

There is something good in everything, I find.
Even in the bad, the agency of mind
reverberates the "might have been."

The backboard forgiving the miss
allows an erring effort to succeed. Oh the bliss
of turning sure defeat to victory. The gun

that didn't fire miraculously spawned a new day,
A gift begun
by the crooked bounce of fate,
or by angels in charge
who may deflect the bullets of life or enlarge

the saving shield. In everything good must prevail
if only as a spark to light the next torch. We must not fail
to expect it, desire it, protect it, nurture it,

that something good…opposite of evil, woven
into life's fabrics for us to discover and benefit.

THE TIP

*My generous, caring wife tried to teach me to leave abundant treasures to waitresses,
but sometimes the girls made it difficult.*

As soon as I receive the slip
my wife says, "Honey, leave a tip.

Now, leave a big one too. That gal
works hard…I'm sure she needs a pal.

She never smiled one time tonight,
so someone has to treat her right."

In shock I start to bite my lip!
Upon my shirt a gravy drip—

on *my* radar she is a blip.
Just why should I leave her a tip?

Dear Wifey notices my gloom
(began when she came in the room

and spilt the water in my lap…
I still can feel my wet fly flap.)

At first I tried to cheer her up,
but when she slopped my coffee cup

I saw her mouth and shoulders droop
until her hair drug through my soup!

I just can't help remembering
my steak looked like some dried up thing,

while I, as hungry as a bear,
had told her, "Make it very rare."
I'm sure it was an anklebone
from some poor starving steer, half grown.

I guess I shouldn't give her blame
for meat that suffered too much flame,

but when she argued, "It *looks* good,"
that wrinkled, tasteless piece of wood

had lost all value to my diet,
it was hard to keep me quiet.

I force myself to grimly smile;
and count my wallet "ones" a while.

I fluff them up to make a pile
look big instead of single file.

It's hard for me to pay her for
incompetence. She makes me sore!

But as I glance at my dear spouse
she winks at me…it's hard to grouse,

to see her pretty, hopeful smile…
I throw some more "ones" on the pile.

And as we leave I hear her quip,
"I'm glad you left a healthy tip."

I AM AN AUTHORITY

Free verse describing a desire to know it all and tell it all. February 11, 2002.

I am an authority. I've always been one…
Just looking for a subject
to fit my knowledge.
It's amazing how many specialized
areas don't cry for my expertise.
With all my preparation, and noting
the exceptional amount of ignorance
in the world, you would think
someone, somewhere, would discover
and use my gifts to enhance their endeavors.
But, then, the advertisement of
my abilities is definitely lacking.
Maybe I need an agent.
I tried to hire my wife, but she didn't cooperate.
She said something about knowing
me too well. Also, she mentioned
that $3.50 an hour did not stimulate
her imagination in my behalf.
Of course, being an authority does have
its drawbacks. Everyone expects so
much of you. Your advice is usually
not heeded even if it's needed.
And if ever required it is more than
likely the middle of the night, or after
their 1st, 2nd, and 3rd choices either
have refused, or are not available.
Then I find it's very difficult to get people
to ask the right questions to match my answers.
Well, at least under the present
circumstances my credentials are seldom
questioned and I never worry about
being wrong because, I am an authority.

Rex B. Valentine

THE WONDER OF HIS POWER, THE POWER OF HIS WORD

I wrote this in August 2007 and published it as a song, but I feel the words should be known as a poem.

He spoke, and lo, the storm was tamed;
the wonder of His power.
Disciples of the Lord were named
by the power of His word.

He spoke, and lo, the lame could walk;
the wonder of His power.
The silent mute began to talk
by the power of His word.

He spoke, and lo, the deaf could hear;
the wonder of His power.
He healed the sick from far and near
by the power of His word.

His voice could be the softest sound
that anyone had heard,
or with His will, could shake the ground
by the power of His word.

As soft as song, or flower, or greatest ever heard;
the wonder of His power, the power of His word.

THE WAITING ROOM
SONNET #10

My daughter, Jenny, was waiting for Conan to be born. I waited in the next room with the family.

Suspense builds in the waiting room
along with hope and drama
not knowing, doubts begin to loom;
when will she be a mama?

I left her for a little while,
she's in the doctor's care.
I still can see her wistful smile
when I walked out of there.

Very soon the nurse will say,
"You have a girl (or boy)."
No matter which it is, today
my heart will fill with joy.

The waiting room, a lonely place.
I just can't wait to see his face.

HARMONY

I started writing about harmony in music, on January 28, 2006, while on our church mission in Bay City, Texas, but realized it is an underused, important word affecting all our lives for good.

Harmony can be served "on the side,"
but a la carte is usually lonely.
Harmony needs to "buddy up" to the bride,
and groom itself to not be "the only."

It can safely come between and strike a chord
of compatibility with upper and lower components.
Harmony really costs very little. Almost anyone can afford
its warm melodiousness of sometimes unseen instruments.

To be effective, harmony must be plural. It has little value alone.
The melody may be beautiful, the bass may boom,
but harmony enhances their union, creating a new tone,
that invades the ear like the breathing in of an exotic perfume.

In football, harmony can foster success when "spreading the field,"
or creating "power formations." One can "have a ball" going between
the center and either end, if they, in harmony, will shield
him, as a first and second floor protect a mezzanine.

The harmony of a chord has its ups and downs.
It is usually a go-between, making use of its ability to give
and integrate its soul to create peace and beautiful sounds.
Harmony is the synergy of song, the comfort and support with which to live.

CEDAR CREEK, THE ENCHANTED STREAM

Cedar Creek runs through land near Oakville, WA. Each year I watch it change from a babbling brook to a wild rushing river and back again. Such beautiful surroundings are there. Written April 12, 2006 on our church mission in Texas. Could I have missed our beautiful streams?

"Is it a river, or a brook?"
The question you might weigh.
The answer rests on when you look,
post winter storms, or summer day.
In winter, water wends its way
with wildly whirling waves.
Its murky torrents on display,
the river misbehaves.

But summer settles like a psalm
and soothes the surging stream.
The rainstorms cease, the skies are calm,
the sun regains its self-esteem.
The brilliance of emerging green
is everywhere you look,
and cutthroat trout are often seen
as they attack a hook.

The water sparkles in the sun,
with beauty clean and clear.
The brook is born. The river done,
till winter sheds its tear.

MY SPIRIT UNCHANGED
SONNET #25

Though we age, our spirit stays the same. However, our body deteriorates, this sonnet explains. Written April 25, 2005.

If I give in, reality will trap
me in this aging body made of clay.
My Spirit hasn't changed. When young I cap-
tured butterflies, found pretty rocks in play.

My school, the world around me, taught me love
and showed me hate, while earthly pressures made
their mark. 'Twas like a shoe, in which you shove
your foot, that's way too small. My spirit paid.

I'm still that same little boy way down inside.
I yearn to shoot a basketball, to run,
to work, to hunt and fish, to hike, to ride.
But age has captured me; reduced my fun.

Still hope, and faith in God revives my soul.
His grace and love will take me to my goal.

FRIED CHICKEN JOY

My mother, Dorothy Valentine, was a wonderful cook. She could make plain food so scrumptious it beat gourmet style.

I remember Sunday dinners
growing up out on the farm.
Dad would kill a fat red hen
that had lost her laying charm.
There was a special axe he used,
and a certain chopping block,
where head removal was the thing,
whether hen or cock.
Then Dad would scald her, pick her feathers;
Mom would dress her out.
She'd warm the old black frying pan
and smear some lard about.
Then roll the chicken parts, fresh cut,
in flour and cracker crumbs,
while in her mind she'd hear us say,
"delicious", with "yum, yums".
She'd peel some red potatoes,
open jars of corn and peas,
that she had canned that autumn
just before the winter freeze.
The fruit room held the big old crock
that cured the sauerkraut.
She'd lift the plate, remove some brine,
and take some "good stuff" out.
She knew the tangy flavor would
enhance the Sunday meal,
with homemade bread and marmalade

spiced up with orange peel.
We kids could hardly wait it out
with pressing hunger pains.
The pleasant, wafting kitchen smells
would permeate our brains.
At last we'd hear the welcome call,
"It's time to come and eat!"
We'd hurry to the dining room
and grab our favorite seat,
(the closest to the chicken plate)
where we would have first choice;
a drumstick or the liver made
a growing boy rejoice.

Now Mother's chicken was <u>so good</u>,
so tasty and so sweet;
'twas fried just right until the bones
released their tender meat.
When Dad had said a thankful prayer
he gave the "go-ahead".
We'd all attack that chicken plate
and grab some home-made bread.

When Mother cautioned, "Save some room",
we knew the reason why,
and all prepared our palates for
her luscious apple pie.

We all now have gone away
to places then unknown;
have seen the world and settled down
with children of our own.
When Sunday comes and we partake
of food someone has praised,
our minds may wander back to see
the home where we were raised.
Yes, Mother's chicken was the best,
she left her legacy.
No one will match her cooking arts,
not even KFC.

SLIPPING FROM WORK TO REST
SONNET #1

Trying to retire brought me great wisdom. Jan. 29, 1998.

To know the secret of a true repose
when batt'ling will, resisting time to rest;
my mind, a door that seems to never close
spews gems of new ideas with great zest.

The muscles of my brain, a state of flex;
why is it? I should revel in the chance
to put my feet up; loosening complex
and choking belts, my freedoms to enhance.

Alas, sometimes I fail to see just why
the motor of my mind keeps running on,
forgetting that the time is passing by
to slip from work to rest before I'm gone.

But God provides no pattern for relief
from life, or work, or love, is my belief.

LEARNING TO MILK EVANGELINE

This was another step in developing a young boy into a productive youth. Written 70 years later on Dec. 9, 2010.

That little baking powder can
I held in my four-year-old hand,
while I squeezed old Evangeline's tit
with the other as I pulled. I wouldn't quit
until the can was nearly full,
and my tiny hand was so tired I couldn't squeeze and pull
anymore. Dad had made for me a little stool
to sit on. Old Evangeline; patient, calm, and cool,
would never lift a foot when I tugged on her
as I learned to milk. The end cow in the line, we were sure
she wouldn't kick or complain no matter how long
I piddled around with her. I could do no wrong.
After a few weeks' mother gave me a bigger pail.
It took me longer but, after a while I didn't fail
to fill that five-pound lard bucket that sat on the concrete floor.
Soon, it too, became too small. I graduated, therefore,
to a twelve quart galvanized mop-pail. Milking with both hands,
I finally learned to finish her within the time demands.
I was passed five by then. Dad and mom were so pleased.
I had developed my little muscles as I pulled and squeezed.
I found a magic in the rhythm when using both hands,
alternating left and right strokes; milk expands
as it covers the bottom of the bucket.
Sounds of the first squirts into the pail echoed like I had struck it.
When first learning to milk, the streams from the teats
would, many times, miss the little pail, and splat on the concrete.
As I practiced each evening, more and more of the warm sweet milk
ended up in the little bucket. Then foam would develop smooth as silk.
As I grew older and stronger milking became a pleasure.
Brother Randy and I became a help to dad, how much was hard to measure.
We all liked to sing as we were milking together,
harmonizing, and keeping the beat

as we pulled and squeezed each teat.
The milking "chores" were a good example of dad's philosophy.
"Always make your work pleasant by having fun;" a lesson to me.

THE MASTER-MIND

In meditating, I realized that man finds that which was made for him to find.

A brilliant star up in the sky-
a brilliant mind to wonder why.
A river flows perpetually
ev'n though it's eaten by a sea.
A bird is flying in the air,
how is man to journey there?
A heart is beating in a chest,
when is the time it comes to rest?
For everything that we uncover,
every thing that we discover
in this world for all mankind
was made ahead for us to find.
Our inspiration's key unlocks
each secret just like building blocks.
Each invention we discover
leads us on to find another.
The patterns we begin to see
were first developed spiritually.
So as we "tune in" with our thoughts,
following the trail of dots
our Maker left for us to find,
we slowly build our Master-mind.
It's plain to see it's one big plan
inspiring wonders "made by man,"
which though they be minute or tall,
man really "made them" not at all.

BE MY GUEST

Jesus Christ's message to us is always there as it was on July 21, 2009.

How many times must I warn you?
How many times can you not hear?
My angels show you what to do,
But penetrate not your ear.

I do not want to let you go;
You're a precious sheep of my fold,
But your spirit, free, says no
to me and your mansion made of gold.

I would take you 'neath my wing
and shelter you from storms.
Oh, child of mine, what is the thing
to which your heart conforms?
Do you not know, I'm just inside
the door; why won't you knock?
I'll open it if you'll abide
with me; there is no lock.

The choices you have made so far,
not always have been best.
Your conscience tells me who you are;
Will you not be my guest?
For I am He who will forgive
those moments in your past,
wherein you slipped and didn't live
my guidelines to the last.

If you repent, I will forget
the times you went astray.
But please forgive yourself, and let
my Spirit have its way.

THE BABYSITTER
SONNET # II

Written while babysitting, grandson Niall Baxter, when he was a few months old, taught me how important a job I had.

There comes a time when I can't be a quitter
Although the pay is quite small.
This is the time; I'm a real baby sitter!
I think I don't mind it at all?

This little guy, like a dynamite cap,
Is really a very small charge.
But it's easy to see when he opens his yap
That his larnyx and his lungs are quite large.

Still, he's a sweetheart, a beautiful boy.
I hope when he reads this someday,
He'll realize his Grandpa's old heart fills with joy
When he throws him a ball when they play.

I guess it's a high-paying job after all.
I'd better be ready; I am. I'm on call.

ALLERGIES

I've been plagued with allergies all my life including chocolate, I'm pretty careful not to consume them, but I'll eat chocolate and itch for a while. Written 11/4/01

Allergies are hard to see,
attacks are quite a mystery.
I'm doing fine and all seems well,
then sneeze so hard it rings my bell.

A pretty girl came in the room
and drifted by with her perfume,
the smell, so heavenly it seemed
was sweeter far than I had dreamed
a woman's scent could ever be;
but she stirred up my allergy.
I have a purring cat at home,
he's gone a lot, he likes to roam.
I pick him up to have some fun
my eyelids itch, my nostrils run.
My wifey dusts and sweeps the floor
but seems to stir the dust up more,
I pinch my nose to crush a sneeze,
and then my lungs begin to wheeze.
Choc'late is my great temptation.
Though I know its devastation.
itching, scratching hives and rash,
in places some would think are brash.

But chocolate is what I crave
until I sometimes misbehave
and gorge myself until I'm ticked
that I'm a chocolate addict.
My allergies—so hard to face
I think I'll leave this human race.
I'll grab a cloud and ride a breeze,
I bet those angels never sneeze.

A SINNER'S LAMENT

We all seem to come short of Gods expectations. (Or our expectations of ourselves.) Written April 13, 2003, forgiveness is important.

Forgive me, Father, for weaknesses I have not overcome.
Forgive me, Father, for leaving when I could have helped someone.

Forgive me, Father, for resting
when I could have risen to your occasion,
but didn't listen to your gentle persuasion.

Forgive me, Father, for not writing down more of the
beautiful thoughts you caused to grace my mind,
those thoughts of giving, healing, loving, helping,
listening, and being kind.

You have listened to my excuses,
overlooked my abuses,
and forgiven me more than seventy times seven.
You've healed my ills.

It gives me chills
to re-experience the dying and undying
love of your Son to lead me to heaven.
Your sacrifice for me was needed.

If only I had always heeded
your still, small voice as it thundered in my ears.
Forgive me, Father, and help me become
one who acts when he hears.

THE BEAUTY OF A WAVE
VILLANELLE #17

Seeing a pretty girl waving so beautifully inspired this villanelle.

Can you express the beauty of a wave?
A friendly gesture coming from the heart?
A frame in time that one would like to save.

You walk along, your countenance is grave.
Your friend will wave and happiness will start.
Can you express the beauty of a wave?

The branches of a tree in wind behave
as if they're greeting you; in beauty part.
A frame in time that one would like to save.

The ocean with its surf, a picture gave
of sparkling water falling all apart.
Can you express the beauty of a wave?

A field of golden grain may cause a rave!
It shimmers in the breeze without a chart.
A frame in time that you would like to save.

A pretty girl, whose hand a man can crave,
might greet and stir him up 'til he's not smart.
Can you express the beauty of a wave?
A frame in time that you would like to save.

THE MIRACLE OF MUSIC
VILLANELLE #6

I love music, this villanelle tells my story.

It's oft been said, "There's music in the air."
How could it be, do melodies have wings?
I've often wondered why I hear them there.

They seem to drift along as on a prayer
and permeate my mind with holy things.
It's oft been said, "There's music in the air."

They say new melodies are very rare,
but in my mind sometimes a new one rings.
I've often wondered why I hear them there.

It seems, of orchestrations I'm aware,
I hear the horns, percussions, bells, and strings.
It's oft been said, "There's music in the air."

Oh, how I wish that everyone could share
the feelings from my soul that burst like springs.
I've often wondered why I feel them there.

The strains of melodies are everywhere.
The spirit of the universe still sings.
It's oft been said, "There's music in the air."
I should not wonder why I hear it there.

ANGEL THOUGHTS

Angel Thoughts expresses my pictures of our guardian angels and what they must go through at times to protect us and serve us.

Can you imagine angel tears that trickle down an angel face?
When I give in to doubts and fears, forget the Savior's loving grace,
I sometimes picture, guarding me, an angel feeling very bad,
whose wings are drooping helplessly, when I deny the aid she had.

I think and see her loving eyes that mirror happiness in me.
At other times she really cries when I behave unrighteously.
I'm sure my angel's not alone. It must be a gigantic task
to monitor, to plan, condone my every thought before I ask.
Such tenderness; to touch my will with pride reduction aptitude,
to humble me, and then instill within my mind a caring mood.

It must be so discouraging to know what I am going to do,
that I might say a hurtful thing, or utter words that are untrue.
I know they have a Godly mind, influencing my every thought
with love and leanings to be kind to those around me as I ought.

Can you imagine loving thoughts that spread a canopy to shield
me from the fire of Satan's plots that bid me weaken, tire, and yield?
Oh Angel Power organized to follow Heav'nly Father's plan;
available and undisguised through prayers of a repentant man.

Can you now see through eyes once blind and hear with understanding ear,
and know with an enlightened mind that angels really do appear?
Oh child of God, they're very real! Surrounding us at ev'ry turn.
We cannot know just how they feel or what they want us all to learn,
but through the Holy Spirit's voice they ride on wings with silent skill
to whisper, sing, and then rejoice when we submit to God, our will.

Rex B. Valentine

OUR FAIR FEATHERED FRIENDS IN FLIGHT

Written April 23, 2010, this poem describes the coordination and magical uniformity of flocks of birds in flight and, in comedy, elevates them above humans in their cooperation in harmonizing public life.

Feathered flight formations flutter, swoop and glide
in perfect harmonic articulation,
as if to give the birdwatchers who hide,
a show; an aerial presentation.

There must be a leader whose signals they follow,
but how do they know to loop low or soar high?
The starlings, the shore birds, the sparrows, or swallow
all move in sharp chorus each time that they fly.

How fun just to know their flight instructor,
to learn of his secret commands.
They dip left, then right. Where is their conductor?
They take off as one, knowing just how he lands.

Amazing, these birds, who were trained as mere babies,
to take off in perfect formation.
And when they come down there is no time for maybes
their landing creates a sensation.

Sometimes they drop in a tree at its top
as the darkness of evening encroaches.
They each choose a branch, landing with a quick stop,
never stuttering with their approaches.

It seems like we mortals could emulate birds,
in peaceful harmonic endeavors.
Instead of lone acts, we could stampede in herds,
or synchronized flocks without feathers.

But few can abide to adhere to a guide

without trying to change his design.
Especially when his name's classified
and they don't know just who to malign.

So we'll follow along, let the birds sing their song,
and marvel at their coordination.
They'll sweep and they'll swoop and maneuver their group
while we humans express fascination.

ESCAPE THE HONEY DOOS
SONNET #23

Every married man has some kind of a "list" from his wife. We have been known to put off doing things as long as possible. I appreciate Diane's very kind and considerate list. It's short as of April 21, 2005.

Retirement is a goal that's on my mind.
Although it hides in crevices of thought,
I dare not let it out, because I find
my wife is planning…and I might get caught.

Right now I know my efforts bring me <u>cash</u>.
If I don't serve my clients it's the worst.
If I retire my schedule will be smashed,
and years of pent-up honey doos come first.

So I've devised a plan that cannot fail.
I'll labor till I'm ninety-one and quit.
I'll grab my wife and hit the travel trail.
We'll sell our place and all the jobs with it.

Then we will cruise and fly the world around,
and settle where no honey doos are found.

HIDDEN GOOD

There is good in everyone. Our job is to find and cultivate it. October 1, 2009.

He was "rough around the edges," so to speak;
some mannerisms not to be desired.
And yet, at times a softness seemed to sneak
into his eyes, which to his heart were wired.
He was raised without a dad and taught by peers.
His life directed by harsh circumstance;
vocabulary filled with filth and sneers;
to be a normal boy he had no chance.

As we conversed I felt his wounded heart
was looking for acceptance, not more hurt.
I did my utmost to become a part
of soul repair, so he could sweep the dirt.

And while we talked a subtle spirit spawned.
He made a conscious effort to refrain
from jarring words who's meaning to him dawned,
offensive, should he take His name in vain.

When mentioning his son there was a brightening.
His countenance showed love and hope and pride.
One could see his vengefulness was lightening.
A change was evident way down inside.
Many like him I have met before,
and searched for goodness as in depth we spoke.
In everyone I'd carefully explore
their interests, trying hard not to provoke.

In every man or woman there is hope
if we encourage them to bring it out.
Sometimes they fight, not knowing how to cope
with love, and are besieged with doubt.
We should not walk away and never try

to find that goodness hidden under pride.
That extra word before we say goodbye
may strike a chord and in their heart abide.

In each event our spirit strives to show
them love, respect, and kindness; it's our test.
Then, when we leave them, in their heart they'll know
we gave, we took the best, and left the rest.

MATURED NOSTALGIA

Those early childhood experiences continue to ring a chord in our minds as adults. Written Dec. 27, 2009.

The train's vibrant whistle wove its way into his dream.
Even in his deep sleep while snoozing in an unfamiliar bed,
in an unfamiliar town, the shrill, shrieking sound didn't seem
to upset or awaken him. A hazy, nostalgic feeling spread
over and around his being. The faint uneven, rumbling roar intertwined
his unconscious thoughts with his active hearing, bringing a well-known
awareness of a pleasant, oft-repeated past experience to his mind.

As his alertness was gradually restored, that same pleasurable, pre-owned
feeling continued to envelope him. Yes, he spent his childhood alongside
a busy railroad track. The trains had come to symbolize
excitement, mystique,
and freedom. They encouraged him to find new lands, to not be satisfied
with the status-quo, but to observe, to dream, to move on, to seek.

OBEDIENCE SPEAKS TO THE HOLY SPIRIT

Obedience helps us control ourselves through the Holy spirit, June 30, 2006.

Obedience, to the Holy Spirit said,
"I hear you," soft and clear.
"Though others doubt, and say that you are dead,
I also feel your presence very near.
Your still, small voice has given men the power
to overcome their yen for 'praise of man',
to realize that every waking hour,
through me, they hear you tell them that they can."

MY FIRST FISH

Growing up on a primitive farm did not allow us many "extras." My parents taught us to innovate and "make do" with what we had. Our special efforts made success even sweeter. April 15, 2010

I didn't have a real fishing pole,
so a vine maple sapling had to do.
At five years old I found a likely hole
right near the river bank with fish in view.
In summertime the river was so clear
the fish were easy seen as they swam by.
And if I stood real still they showed no fear,
but watched me from the corner of their eye.
I talked my mother into taking me
down to the river to teach me to fish.
My dad cut the 8 foot pole from a tree,
while Mom found a hook and line in a dish
she kept out on the fruit room shelf.
They put it together and used an iron nut

as a sinker weight, which I myself
thought looked quite crude. I was worried, but,
I was thrilled when Mother baited my hook
with a squiggly worm that we found in a seam
'neath old boards near the barn. Then Mother took
the vine maple pole and swung the bait out in the stream.
She handed me the pole. As the nut for a weight
slowly found its way to the bottom of an eddy,
the worm on the hook floated free. That bait
danced enticingly around a fish, who was ready
for dinner, but very cautious. Slowly he slipped
his big sucker mouth over the worm on the hook,
then quickly turned to escape. Instinctively I flipped
my short pole back, and like the storybook
ending pictured strong in my mind,
the big 17 inch fish flew over my head
and landed and flopped on the bank just behind.
Mother acted quickly, for he wasn't dead,
and kept him from flipping right back in the stream.
I was very excited that I had caught a fish!!
It seemed that I might still be in a dream
till I touched it! It was real now, not just a wish.
And though an old sucker has too many bones to eat,
Mother fried it beautifully at my urging.
But if memory serves me, there were more bones than meat,
which kept us from gorging and splurging.

TIME AFTER TIME AFTER TIME
SONNET #12

We never seem to learn from the past. We just keep making the same mistakes all though history.

Each generation does live of itself
in spite of the records before.
If only its books would remove from the shelf
to inspire and instruct from the yore.

Problems do test us again and again,
some answers are written in blood.
Why do we not listen like Noah did when
he was warned of the terrible flood.

Somehow we manage, we stumble and fall,
repeat time worn woes and mistakes.
Remaking discoveries, but through it all
we bind up our wounds, soothe our aches.

"Learn by experience," a phrase we revere,
o'er looking the past we just charge on from here.

ATTITUDE
VILLANELLE #11

Written while on our church mission in Texas, soon after arriving in Bay City, it discusses the importance of our attitude and our moods. 8/21/2005.

One key affecting life is attitude.
Our outlook can dishearten, or inspire.
Our influence is governed by our mood.

When love is present, evil is subdued.
Unselfish love may calm a raging ire.
One key affecting life is attitude.

Some people hold their thoughts in solitude,
afraid to speak lest they be judged a liar.
Our influence is governed by our mood.

When standing for the right our lives exude
the fearlessness that others can admire.
One key affecting life is attitude.

Our point of view can conjure up a feud,
if we allow contention to transpire.
Our influence is governed by our mood.

A happy frame of mind, we may conclude,
can bring about and feed a heart's desire.
One key affecting life is attitude.
Our influence is governed by our mood.

WAITING

Much of our life involves waiting for someone or something. This poem expresses my feelings about it.

It seems as if we're waiting, waiting,
waiting all our lives.
When we are three it's irritating
'til we get our trikes.

But then three wheels becomes "old hat,"
we can't wait for our bikes.
While riding them the tires go flat,
which sometimes spawn hitch-hikes.

It's hard to wait for our first car
and drivers license too,
for our first date, to travel far ,
do what we want to do.

It seems our lives are waiting games,
we long for things untried .
We search for riches, love, and fame,
we're never satisfied.

And all our lives we're waiting, waiting
for that something new.
But we must keep anticipating
making dreams come true .

UNRAVELING RHYME
SONNET #21

Rhyme was once the king style of poetry, but now free verse and broken ideas and thoughts are popular. Rhyming structured poetry is much harder to perfect and promote the camaraderie of spirits, but well worth the extra effort.

The plight of man recorded on a page;
the stories told by one who sees or knows
can touch with rhythm, endless minds engage,
and stir the souls with rhyming words not prose.

A metered rhyme denotes a fading time
when structure was important to success,
but prose has liberated thinking minds,
allowing thoughts extemporaneous.

The "life is easy" mindset took its toll
in splintered lines and thoughts with hanging phrase,

until, to be uncivilized is goal
for writers' broken views and simple ways.

The abstract thoughts that follow no design,
might bring results like drinking too much wine.

THE "COW-TOW"

Cattle have been a part of my life all my life.
Women could learn a lot from bovine mothers.

The young mother with her first calf, befuddled by responsibility
never before encountered; no previous instruction, no tutoring.
New life is entrusted to an untried matriarch, who had always followed
her mother who was now disinterested in the daughter.

The older mother had a new offspring of her own to train.
The bovinal discipline of her mother's new baby, a yearly practiced art,
was poetry in motion. Her mother's baby calf, responding to her every
nosing nudge, lick of her rough tongue, or murmuring moo,
was the epitome of a cow's maternal success.

Her older daughter, the young mother, trailed bewilderedly
after <u>her</u> calf as it ran around helter-skelter. Her desperate
mooing seemed to have no effect on her 24-hour old offspring,
as many young, and sometimes older women "cow-tow" to their
children, experiencing the same effect.

They ask their young ones what they want over and over again
'til their children, who haven't a clue how life should unfold,
are running the show, with their mothers chasing after them
trying to please their every whim instead of the
mother taking control and directing her baby into positive paths;
teaching it the discipline it will need when old enough to

make decisions on its own.
The young bovine mother will soon learn how to control her
newly born calf, which she will lovingly raise.

She will learn to communicate her better judgment of actions to her baby,
which will help it enjoy companionship of other calves, protect it from
predators, and allow it proper exercise, as she nurses it along to maturity.
So many women could learn so much if they could study
and understand the methods and successes of so-called dumb animals.

CHRISTMAS CHEER, NOW IT'S HERE

Christmas is a very special time. These thoughts came flooding into me while waiting for Diane on Dec. 22, 2008 to finish her shopping.

As I'm writing this, the snow is swirling 'round my car.
It's almost Christmas, and I wonder if it's snowing where you are?
There is a freshness in the air, especially when it stops,
except for chimneys here and there and smoky chimney tops.

They tell a different story indicating warmth and love.
I wonder who the people are and what they're dreaming of?
Diane is shopping while I write, her list goes on and on,
but she enjoys it, and she will, until her money's gone.

I know she makes provisions for this time throughout the year
and she will have enough for all to share our Christmas cheer.
She is a special woman, wife, and mother in her roles;
to many children, grands and greats, a helper with their goals.

These Christmas times bring out the best in people as a rule.
With love and caring in the air it's harder to be cruel.
Christmas is a magic time, and children everywhere
are trying hard to prove they're good and sometimes say a prayer,

that Santa will remember them and bring their heart's desire.
This is the time they do their best to do what we require.
Under all, our Savior's birth becomes more real to us.
We worship him without fanfare, with no commercial fuss.

The Holy Ghost that he sent when leaving us behind
will serve us well if we will keep a clean and loving mind.

COMFORT
SONNET # 33

Comfort is so important to our beings, and can give us pure joy. Aug. 8, 2007.

Comfort after hurt or sorrow
gives us strength to live tomorrow;
though our pain is fresh today,
comfort pushes it away.

Comfort does have many faces,
coming from unusual places.
Sometimes it is but a glance,
made by someone just by chance.

It can be a soothing bath,
or walking down a garden path.
When one breathes the breath of grief
an air of solace gives relief.

Comfort fills so many roles
and through His love, redeems our souls.

AUSTRALIAN HSINKU

At the World Congress of Poets convention in Tai'an, China in October 2005, Dr. Kenneth Fan from Taiwan introduced a "new" type of poem called the "Hsinku". They must have 4 lines of any length. The 2nd and 4th lines must rhyme. The 4th line should be a surprise ending, or give it an unusual twist or ending.

The Australian dove into the sea,
afraid of the lightning and thunder.
When he didn't come up, they said,
"Let him be;
he's used to being down under."

FROG HSINKU

The Frog Hsinku won 5th place at the 2009 convention in Nicaragua.

The frog fell in the pond.
I could see that he was soaked.
But then he went beyond.
To my surprise, he croaked.

WHY HIS SONG WAS LONG

I wrote this in China and it was judged first place of the Hsinku poems in 2005.

The trumpet player tooted his song
it went on from night to morn.
The cowboy explained it was the "Cattle Call"
and he was using a real Long-horn.

THE HOUSE WITH A PURPLE DOOR
VILLANELLE #13

My little 4 year old grandson, Harrison Tintle, moved from the Washington D.C. area to near Salt Lake City with his parents. The resulting Villanelle recounts his feelings, and won 3rd place in the Famous Poets' competition in 2007 and a free publishing contract for a book. Written June 19, 2007.

In the eyes of the world, it was just a shack,
the little house with a purple door.
He said, "Mama, when are we going back?"

They had left their home by the railroad track
about a year before.
In the eyes of the world it was just a shack.

His mother was suddenly taken aback
by the little boy about four.
He said, "Mama, when are we going back?"

They had bought a big house with a lot of jack,
but that purple door house he adored.
In the eyes of the world it was just a shack,

but to him, it was a home without lack,
where they lived by the track before.
He said, "Mama, when are we going back?"

He started to pack his little backpack
to return to his home, oh so poor.
In the eyes of the world it was just a shack;
he said, "Mama, when are we going back
to my house with a purple door?"

THE SAVOR OF HIS SALT

My dad always had a plan for me, but I had to find my own.

The time it takes to learn to work will vary man to man.
For early on we tend to shirk our task each time we can.

The motivators in our lives can come at any age.
A Dad cajoles, or pleads, or drives his babes 'til they engage

their untried talents in pursuit of goals for them *he's* set.
He hopes his children won't refute his dreams, or show regret.

So many times a father fails; relives his life through them,
considers not his own coattails do have a different hem.

But still, the value of his guide through life is easy seen.
Especially if love abides at times he might demean.

So when the child is old enough, his mind and heart to know,
sometimes the way is very rough, he knows not where to go.

He wants to fill his Dad's desire, to please his every whit.
But doing so would then require he change his life a bit.

Oh destiny, oh fate of star, how does he ever cope?
Oh voiceless God, how near or far, can you renew his hope?

The discipline his father taught will serve him well today.
Though different, the road to walk may lead another way.

His father's life a stepping stone, his love a catapult,
propels him on, he'll be his own, the savor of his salt.

OH WINTER DAY
SONNET #15

I love warm, long summer days. This sonnet explains, we must accept the unpleasant with the pleasant. Written on or about the longest day of the year, June 22, 2003.

Oh winter day, how short from dawn to dark!
I must encourage, coax you to begin,
for when I rise to stroll through field and park
I wait impatiently for light to win.

You hurry not, your sun seems lazy, slow
to break the tether of the sleeping night.
And when, oh winter day, you have to go,
you slip through dusky curtains out of sight.

I dream of longer days. Though slow to come,
they gain momentum from the scheme of things.
Then poof! it's summer solstice, hot the sun!
But you'll not stay the longer day. No strings

can hold you when you seek a little rest;
retreat to a repeat, that you know best.

DEERS IS SCARED, BUT BEARS IS NOT

Wise words from my little grandson, Liam Baxter five years old when questioned, 7/16/04.

There are those times when backing up
beats recklessly charging ahead.
Also, times when shutting your mouth
beats eating the words you said.

If your opponent has more clout
it's time to vacate the ring.
If you are angry you might want to shout,
but it may be smarter to sing.

Here's how a five year old captures this thing.
The deer sneaked into our yard one day
to nibble on apples and pears.
We sent out our grandson to chase them away,

which he did with daring fanfares.
We asked if he'd frighten the animals off
if he saw there were bears in our yard.

His eyes grew in size, he choked back a cough;
to control his emotions was hard.
Some children talk, no words are spared…

that five year old sage gave this thought:
"When you're in the woods, the deers is scared,
but bears--? But bears is not!"

POET OF FAME
SONNET #28

This sonnet #28 written November 5, 2005 in Bay City, Texas on our church mission explains my desire to perfect my trade in which "there is no norm. "The proof is in the pudding."

To be a poet of renown,
his mind may spawn contortions,
and see some things as upside-down,
or balanced strict proportions.

In poetry there is no norm,
no named denominations.
The gifted writer chooses form
that fits his new creations.

His thoughts and motives leave his pen,
extensions of his notions.
In innovative phrase, his yen
is sharing his emotions.

To garner fame, or great renown
his works will gain his poet's crown.

BEAUTIFUL, I THINK
SONNET #26

All seem to have a different idea of what is beautiful. It is a good thing. This is what I thought on April 27, 2005.

Why can't we all see beauty everywhere,
each face a pleasing sight for all who see?
What causes us to love brown eyes, red hair?
Or stand in awe of flowers or a tree.

Some say that beauty is a state of mind.
That it is governed by whose eyes behold.
And then, there are the ones who'd never find
a thing of beauty should it be pure gold.

All beauty is not visual, one may hear
it both in music and a kindly voice.
It may be tasted, smelled, or felt, it's clear,
but beauty lives in a beholders choice.

One's heart and mind must feel and view in sync
for something to be beautiful, I think.

ALMOST HOME

So many times while driving a car, I almost went to sleep. I forced myself to stay awake and get home to my lovely wife and family. Written on 9/26/04 after a close call.

Home seems so far away
only 90 miles
must keep awake
the freeway straight and monotonous
blends into a dream I might
normally have this time of night
suddenly a comet slices thru
my vision as the almost
formed dream evaporates from
the adrenaline rush…
just another headlight.
Thank you God!
Buttocks straightened, reset in
adjustable seat
re-grip steering wheel
wide awake now
won't let that happen again.
Road so smooth, comfortable
car, all is well.
A transparent veil of contentment sweeps
over my mind, becoming a
powerful soul assuaging sedative, soothing
my senses

my subconscious mind sees
the road without reporting
to the other me
that is weakened by my rational loving thoughts
of home and family-
so glad when home.

What's that thumping?
I'm knocking on my door
"It's me honey"
No! It's the warning bumps
at road edge-
I'm going off the highway!
Dreamy images quickly
snap into focus-
Whew!
Just missed that bridge railing
wide awake now!
Thank you again, Dear God.
I was almost home.

JEALOUSY
SONNET #16

Sometimes I have a tendency to be jealous of my beautiful wife, Diane. But my possessiveness evaporates when I remember how true she has always been. We free each other to be ourselves. Written 8/29/03.

Oh, how do I refrain from jealousy?
That monster! It attacks my blinded side.
It wounds me, twists me, spawns repellency
from her, whom I have taken for a bride.

Impacts of competition are so strong
I desper'tly inject compellency. When
freedom would promote a lover's song
I foster a return of jealousy.

The remedy won't take a scholar's book,
or volumes written by the world's renown's.
No, it is found within my lover's "look,"
her actions, words of trust, that have no bounds.

So thank you, God, for giving her to me,
with love so true. No need for jealousy.

LOVE NEVER FAILETH

The love of God is constant. If we make ourselves available to it, it will not fail us. Written December 31, 2002.

The rain is freely slicing through
the heavy open air.
I stand under a sheltering fir tree,
partially shielded
until the branches, absorbing water,
are saturated.
As they ripple in a gusting breeze
they seem to burst into tears
and shower me.
My worldly shelter has failed.
But you, O Lord, provide a cover for me
if I stand in Holy Places,
allowing your loving arms to encircle me.
Your celestial breezes refresh my soul
with dew from Heaven.
By your grace, I am eternally

safe in your love.
The pure love of Christ
never faileth.

A VILLANELLE! YOU CAN'T TELL?
VILLANELLE #15

A little nonsense in villanelle fun form, written June 21, 2007.

I'm writing you this Villanelle
I'll camouflage its style,
so you can hardly ever tell

it when you read this Villanelle,
till you have pondered it awhile.
I'm writing you this Villanelle,

and trying hard to make it jell.
Remember this is just a trial,
so you could hardly ever tell

until it rings your mem'ry bell
and stirs up your awareness while
I'm writing you this Villanelle.

Since I have finally learned to spell
the dictionary's in a pile.
So you could hardly ever tell,

because these words will never sell.
By now I hope I've made you smile.
I'm writing you this Villanelle,
but don't you ever, ever tell.

THE WONDER OF LOVE
VILLANELLE #9

In thinking of my wonderful mate, Diane, I wrote this villanelle #9 for her in May 2005.

My love, you are so beautiful to me.
Your pretty eyes just sparkle when you smile.
No wonder you're the only one I see.

Our private moments are so heavenly.
You show me love, you make my life worthwhile.
My love, you are so beautiful to me.

Our vows to serve each other are the key,
enticing each to go the extra mile.
No wonder you're the only one I see.

It's often that we seem to disagree,
but never place the other one on trial.
My love, you are so beautiful to me.

If I am ever lost I hope I'll be
alone with you on some deserted isle.
No wonder, you're the only one I'd see.

I love your heart, I love your thoughts, and style.
We seem to compliment so perfectly.
My love, you are so beautiful to me.
No wonder you're the only one I see.

SEEK POWER OF PERPETUAL PERFECTION

If I "allow myself to know", looking and listening to the spiritual guidance around me, I progress in every area. Written February 1998-revised April 2009.

Does the world revolve around you?
Or, do you float in a sea—polluted with indecision,
misunderstanding, self-pity, and sorrow?

Or are you on a course directed by others
of high velocity, high sideboards, with
no place to land if you jump.

If you can watch the sun, ascending
from morning's shadowy dawn, as it
breaks away from earth's glowing rim,

traveling silently across the sky, to escape
in a glorious blaze, the watchful eye of day,
you may understand the precise power

of heaven's amazing perpetual perfection.
The success of personal power and an organized life
is available to all who plan under the Great planner's
direction.

As the watch-stem is the directing core of time,
so shall the Great Planner stabilize your efforts
with the Heart of all hearts, and mind of all minds.

Link your heart and mind to the center of all knowledge
and intelligence, allowing the world to revolve
around you, guiding you toward amazing perpetual perfection.

A BLOSSOM OF SPRING

"A Blossom of Spring" came to me on March 15, 2004 as I realized the beauty of flowering springtime. Then, in meditating, the blossom became much, much, more than beauty. Its generative power almost overwhelmed me. I guess it isn't so delicate after all.

A blossom is surely a delicate thing;
a sensitive harbinger looking for spring.

Its petals are packed in a bud on a stem
'til they burst from their prison, a colorful gem.

Encouraged by sunlight, it beckons the bees
as they search for sweet nectar in flowers and trees.

A blossom is awesome, a beautiful sight,
in sunlight exploding, then hiding at night.

When Jack Frost approaches it cowers with fear.
In heavy cold rains it sheds many-a-tear.

When blustery winds blow its petals apart,
it sighs and it cries, and exposes its heart.

The life of a blossom is measured in hours,
for under its beauty it's swelling with powers,

developing into a fluff or a fruit,
or a seed, or a pod, or a life giving shoot.

It is borne of a thought of a flower or tree
that bursts with a passion and felicity.

Precursor of fruit and a herald of spring;
a blossom **may not be** a delicate thing.

MUSIC AND FLIGHT
SONNET #27

While flying from Chicago to Beijing for the World congress of Poets convention I wrote this during the 13+ hour nonstop flight on October 25, 2005.

When on a musical journey,
relax, just kick back and wing it.
If the music is good, be part of the flight,
you won't even have to sing it.

As you listen be ready for take-off.
It's one time you loosen your belt.
The mood of the tune can be like a balloon,
it will lift up and soar, with the brake off.

Music can be such a transport,
to take you right out of this world.
Your cares may all die; your spirits may fly
in a breeze like a flag that's unfurled.

Music can raise you to heights
that will rival a plane in its flights.

THE ADDRESS BOOK

After my mother passed away, I found her old address book. This poem won first place internationally for rhyming poetry at the 2009 convention in Nicaragua for the World Congress of Poets.

In looking through possessions held and cherished many years,
I saw the names so deftly spelled among her souvenirs.
The address book was tattered, torn; it's binding loose and stripped.

So old, its index tabs were worn from hands whose fingers gripped.

At first I tossed it on the pile of things to throw away.
But after just a little while it beckoned me to stay.
I picked it up, sat down to rest, and opened it again.
It seemed that God my efforts blessed, I gazed upon my name.

The page was smudged from many calls and teardrops, I could tell.
She didn't always share her falls, or tell me when she fell.
Her thoughts and prayers had always been for those she loved and served.
From newborn babe to aging man, 'twas more than I deserved.

Yes, there were many other names within that tattered book.
I scanned the pages, said a prayer, then I began to look
at all her friends who'd gone before, in mem'ry some I'd known.
'Twas then I realized much more why she had felt alone.

A line was neatly penciled through the names when they had died.
"Deceased" was written by them too, and droplets where she cried.

Oh Mother, what a loving soul you were. I miss you so.
I know you're on the Savior's roll, you had not far to go
to meet Him at His throne on high; your mansion He's prepared.
Your crown of glory now is nigh because you loved and cared.
The tattered address book, I'll keep, with names of friends you knew.
Then someday in my final sleep I'll meet them all, with you.

TELL A VISION
(VERSION 2)

On our church Mission we didn't have the television, so we visited a lot and so enjoyed each other. 2/20/06

Can you "Tell a Vision" of your mind's chromatic screens?
Entwine your mind with others when portraying vivid scenes?
The art of story telling is as varied as the sand.
Some tales may be most interesting when they're told firsthand.
Sometimes it helps, when in the mood, to narrate in the dark,
where pictures form within your head from colorful remark.
There is no competition there, from garish shades of light,
so you can "Tell a Vision," color film, or black and white.

Thoughts can come together, dreams can be projected then,
without the opposition of a why, or how, or when.
Rivers deep, become small streams, steep mountains, gentle slopes.
Hidden tears and silent prayers may stimulate new hopes.
It may be reminiscing that can take the center stage
with memories so vivid, though attained at early age.
Some visions are so personal, it's better you forget,
those open deeds of bygone shame like video cassette.
Still better, "Tell a Vision," that beholds a new-made man,
where God has intervened and life has taken on a plan.
Though new, it is a story told so many times of yore,
where one sees hope o'ercome the doubts that plagued a life before.

Describe the joy that love inflames, when hearts are linked as one.
Convey the image of a chain to God and to his Son.
There power flows continually from Father at the top
to you and to all other links of virtue, it's non-stop.
"Tell a Vision" of His love o'er-powering greed and lust.
Paint a picture of a King whose rule is fair and just.
Illustrate your cinema with words of heart; be bold.
Yes, "tell your vision" of 'The Greatest Story Ever Told'.

Rex B. Valentine

THE BIKE WITH FOUR FEET

My brother Randy and I pooled our pennies when I was five & a half and he was four. The little bicycle we wanted cost $26.00. We dumped our money jar out on the counter, and the shop proprietor counted and counted. We were about $8.00 short, and were becoming sad and dejected until our daddy pulled out the other $8.00 and we got the tiny bike after all. We couldn't wait to learn to ride it.

You may have heard the saying, "Push the pedal to the metal,"
   but as little boys, when playing, we'd settle on the pedals.
You see, we could afford only one bike; it was a tiny one at that.
And when we headed for a place we liked, we adopted an unusual format.
The roads were rough with a gravel base, so bicycles weren't a smooth ride.
But when we rode to cousin Karl's place, we couldn't ride side by side.
     I sat on the seat of that tiny machine,
     while on the pedals Randy would stand.
     My feet were with his, an unusual scene,
     as the pedals with four feet were manned.
     Cousin Karl's place was three miles away
     and we had so much fun when we played,
that we pestered our mom to spend the whole day and more,
     if we could have stayed.
But just before dusk, we would start down the road to
     get home before it was dark.
We'd pump on those pedals and reach our abode
     just in time for the song of the lark.
That bike was a small one, but we didn't care, we'd
     jump on when ready to go.
Four feet on the pedals, we soon would be there,
     yes, Randy and I were not slow.
That cute little bike was a blessing to us; we rode it wherever we went.
   Though comforts were few, we'd not make a fuss;
     each travel a pleasant event.

PRESERVE BEAUTY

I saw this tiny, single stemmed pansy bloom poking up through a crack in the concrete. I'm a sucker for pansies. I think they are gorgeous. This poem was judged second of 405 entries at the State Grange Poetry contest in June, 2011. Written June 30, 2007.

The little pansy poked its pretty face
up through the concrete crevice on the walk.

It's singleness of purpose filled the space,
a tiny crack made for one spindly stalk.

Now why would nature send its beauty queen
to grace a graying path of cement stone,

where careless eyes might miss the lovely scene
and careless feet its royalty dethrone?

The Lord of beauty, love, and elegance,
is not particular where sows his seeds.

A drab and dingy place he might enhance
with lovely flowers 'mid the grisly weeds.

So little purple pansy hold your ground.
May beauty be a beacon to your place,

that all who pass go carefully around
and see the smile upon your pretty face.

Were all written on July 20, 2011. I tried to capture important views of special words.

HINDSIGHT

It's easier when looking back
to see what might have been,
than springing forward from the pack
to do it now, not then.

LEADERSHIP

Good leadership will never be
a part of what you do
until as follower, you see
the guiding light that's leading you.

PERSISTANCE

Persistence is a virtue when
our goal is worthy of
repeated efforts serving men
and blessed by Father's love.

THE PRUNER

As a lover of fruit trees and youth I have watched as my orchardist literally transforms ill-shapen trees to ones of beauty with excellent fruit. Also, I've spent great spaces of my life encouraging youth "at risk" to seek a better, more productive life. Hence, this poem, which won first place internationally in the rhyming category at the Conference of the World Congress of Poets in Larissa, Greece in July of 2011. Note that each line is double rhymed (in the middle and at the end). Written March 6, 2010.

The limbs of the half-grown apple tree were grotesque at their best.
The orchard owner didn't see and prune it like the rest.
It sat alone; had never grown the way of other trees
that he had planted row by row and shaped them; eyes to please.
The tangled mess of branches fought their way to see the light.
Till they had hurt themselves, were caught with nothing growing right.
And then one day the orchardist thought he'd remove the tree.
He'd cut it down with axe he brought, "It won't be missed," thought he.
It's apples, tiny, not the size the market did require.
The orchardist had deemed it wise the tree should just expire.
He raised his axe to cut it down but something made him stop.
He looked it over, once around from bottom to the top.
"Oh, what if I remove the wood? (some limbs it doesn't need);
to shape the tree 'til it looks good. It's from the choicest seed."
So he began to prune and trim until the task was done.
It seemed the tree smiled back at him, as it soaked in the sun.

Next year the apples on the tree were bigger than before.
And each succeeding year would see it ripen more and more.
The tree is like an untrained youth whose life is "on the line".
Though he be rash, at times uncouth, and no one's valentine,
when pruned by love and discipline sometimes he will respond.
If in the light his heart is won, to goodness he will bond.
Sometimes we overlook a jewel whose life's a tangled mess?
Who really won't be mean and cruel if we show love, and bless.
So let us watch and be aware of those who most reject,
and ready be to "just be there" to show them our respect.
They, like the tree, will blossom more when pure light filters in.
And help them prune the dross before they're cut off; lost to men.

www.ingramcontent.com/pod-product-compliance
Lightning Source LLC
Chambersburg PA
CBHW052156110526
44591CB00012B/1968